Raising Champions

A Parent's Role in Sports

TOM TOPAUM

ISBN 979-8-9999882-0-1 *(paperback)*
ISBN 979-8-9999882-1-8 *(ebook)*

Book design: meadencreative.com

Contents

Introduction

A Promise Once Held

When I was 16 years old and a junior in high school, a scout with the San Francisco Giants Professional Baseball Organization offered me the chance to sign as a free agent and finish high school by earning a GED. At the time, I was ranked among the top high school baseball players in the country. Colleges from across the nation were calling with full scholarship offers, and nearly every professional scout I met told me I was a lock for the top 10 rounds of the Major League Draft.

But just a year after the conversation with the Giants, everything changed. I injured my shoulder, and just like that my future took a hard turn. Oddly enough, I felt a strange sense of relief. The constant pressure to succeed in baseball finally eased. My parents, on the other hand, were devastated. They felt like years of sacrifice, focus, and relentless training had been washed away in a single moment. It was as if someone in the family had died. There was no backup plan. Everything had been built around the hope of playing professional baseball.

Despite the injury, I kept playing and was eventually drafted by the Giants in 1995. I signed a professional contract and entered the Giants Minor League System, but the dream didn't unfold the way any of us had expected. That experience would go on to shape how I've seen sports, pressure, identity, and purpose ever since.

Growing Up Under Pressure

I grew up in a home where the walls echoed with high expectations, and the drive to win never took a day off. I was raised to believe that greatness wasn't a gift, it was a choice you made every day when no one was watching. Winning wasn't optional and giving anything less than everything was considered failure. Every team practice, every (daily) training session at home, and every game was treated like a championship. Mistakes had consequences. Success was demanded. Pressure was constant.

That environment shaped me. It sharpened my competitive edge and fueled a work ethic that extended far beyond my youth playing days. I still consider those experiences a cornerstone of much of the success I've experienced in life. But it also came with a cost.

The relentless pursuit of perfection left little room for joy, freedom, or simply being a kid. I learned to equate my worth with my performance and to fear mistakes more than I valued growth. And as I've watched countless young athletes and their parents carry the same silent weight I once did, I've come to see how thin the line really is between pushing a child to be their best and pushing them too far.

Life Beyond Sports

The values instilled in me early on laid the groundwork for my career beyond sports. For over two decades, I worked as a professional investigator, with 18 of those years in law enforcement, where I focused primarily on violent crimes. I served in various investigative roles, including Criminal Intelligence, Major Crimes, and as a member of an FBI Task Force. During that time, I was also a certified polygraph examiner, conducting examinations and interrogations as part of my investigative responsibility. I later transitioned to the private sector, where I now work as an investigations manager for a Fortune 500 company, working closely with law enforcement to investigate organized crime groups that target and threaten the global supply chain.

A career in professional investigations is high-pressure, unpredictable and filled with long hours, critical decisions, and unexpected turns that demand discipline, resilience, and the ability to perform under stress. What prepared me for this life wasn't just the training or experience I gained in the job. It was the foundation built during my years as a young athlete. Sports taught me how to handle adversity, how to be part of a team pursuing a common goal, and how to stay mentally tough in the face of setbacks.

From an early age, I approached everything like a competition. I came to believe there's no substitute for hard work, dedication, and perseverance. Winning wasn't just about coming out on top, it was about doing everything in my power to give my absolute best, every single time. That drive didn't stop when the games ended; it followed me into my career.

Coaching and Parenting

While advancing professionally, I poured just as much time and energy into my second calling: coaching. For years, I balanced both worlds with a passion to mentor, lead, and develop athletes at every level. Coaching wasn't just something I did on the side; it was, and still is, a core part of who I am.

But while my athletic background and professional career shaped how I coached, **it was parenting that gave me the deepest insight.** I was no longer just guiding other people's kids; I was raising my own athletes, too.

At the same time I was coaching young athletes, I was watching my children grow and navigate the world of sports. I was a parent in the stands, living through every high and low, win and loss, just like so many others. Over the years, I have interacted closely with countless parents, hearing their hopes, frustrations, and struggles as they tried to do what was best for their children. All those experiences gave me a 360-degree view of youth sports, from the field, the bench, and the bleachers, and shaped how I understand and value the vital role parents play in their child's athletic journey.

Growing up, I spent countless hours training on fields, courts, in athletic facilities, and even in my garage, which was stocked with exercise equipment. I played multiple sports every year, often overlapping with each other. My whole world revolved around sports, which taught me discipline, commitment, and how to push through obstacles.

Along the way, my father, a coach in his own right, was always pushing me to do better. His expectations were high, and the pressure he placed on me was undeniable. From the outside looking in, I'm sure it appeared the pressure he put on me wasn't just intense, it was overwhelming. To outsiders, it would not have looked like a father simply pushing his child to be great, but more like a father causing emotional strain and maybe even being borderline abusive. At the time, I didn't fully understand that his overbearing nature came from a place of deep care and a desire to see me succeed. Now, looking back as a father and a coach myself, I know that everything he did came from believing in me and his desire to see me become someone great.

Fast forward to today, and I've had the privilege of coaching athletes across youth levels, high school varsity teams, and Division III college athletics. In addition, each of my children has navigated their own sports journey, two of them playing soccer at the Division I and Division II levels. I understand firsthand the intricacies of being a parent in sports, both in the moment and down the road - the balancing act between wanting the best for your child and recognizing the realities of what sports are truly about for them.

Why This Book?

In *Raising Champions: A Parent's Role in Sports*, I want to share everything I've learned through these multiple lenses, first as an athlete, then as a coach, and finally, as a parent. I'll be honest with you: the path is not always clear, and the road is not always smooth. As parents, we often walk a fine line between motivating our children and respecting their autonomy, between pushing them toward success and allowing them to find their own way. We want them to thrive in the moment, to win, to be great, to be "the best," but we also want them to gain something deeper, something that will stay with them for life, regardless of any degree of success and accolades they experience along the way.

Participating in a sport is not just about the game, but about the people we become through those experiences. Whether your child is just starting out or aspires to have a professional career, it's crucial to remember that sports are about much more than their position on the coach's depth chart or the outcome of individual games or seasons. Being active in a sport offers opportunities for growth, for life lessons, and for personal development that last long after the final game is played.

In this book, I use stories, lessons, and challenges I've encountered in my life to help you manage the complex dynamics of raising a child in sports, to support them through the highs and lows, to reconcile your desires for their success with their own, and to understand what sports are likely doing for them in the present, as well as how they can aid them in their future. I'll show you how to balance ambition with enjoyment, success with mental well-being, and competition with character-building.

Christian pastor, author and spiritual mentor A.W. Tozer wrote, "The only book that should ever be written is one that flows up from the heart, forced out by the inward pressure." He said a true message doesn't come from ambition, but from burden. That's how this book began. I didn't set out to write a book about youth sports. I set out to write a book about the heart of a young person growing up in a sports-driven world and how we, as parents, have the power to either shape it or (unintentionally) crush it.

If there's one thing I've learned over the years, it's this: While successful people grow through their personal experience, those who achieve the highest levels of success also learn from the experiences of others. My hope is that as you read this book, you'll not only see my journey, but find clarity, hope, and wisdom in your own, as you walk the path of raising a champion.

A Special Note to the Reader

Every family's journey through youth and high school sports looks different. This book is written to resonate with parents from all backgrounds, including those whose upbringing was very different from mine or who didn't grow up in a traditional environment.

As you begin reading, I want to first acknowledge that not everyone grew up with supportive or involved parents, whether in sports or in life. I'm sure many of you were left to figure things out on your own. Others had to lean on a coach, mentor, or friend to find guidance and direction.

Maybe you received very little encouragement growing up, or perhaps the guidance you did receive came with pressure, unrealistic expectations, or emotional baggage. You might carry regrets about missed opportunities or simply wonder how things might've turned out differently if you'd had the right support.

Whatever your story, I believe this book will give you insight, tips and reflection points.

You might be parenting in a divided home, where one parent is fully engaged and the other is disconnected or absent. Maybe you're carrying the weight of both roles and trying to fill the emotional, spiritual, and practical gaps left by a parent who 'isn't there.' You may be a single parent doing your best with limited time and energy, a stepparent learning how to support with both care and humility, or a parent who never played sports yourself, so is unsure how to help your child move through this world.

You may also be a devoted, present parent who doesn't consider sports a top priority. Maybe you place a greater emphasis on academics, faith, or family time, and sometimes worry that your lack of enthusiasm for athletics is misunderstood. That perspective matters, too. Your values shape your priorities. This book isn't here to override those, but rather to show how sports can offer powerful lessons and opportunities for growth in ways you might not currently realize.

This is not a book about parenting perfectly. It's about showing up intentionally for your child, and for yourself. It's about growing, learning, and finding grace as you lead your family through the often intense and emotional world of youth sports.

Whether you're starting from scratch, eager to parent differently from the way you were raised, or simply looking for a new perspective, I hope this book encourages you and equips you with something valuable to carry forward.

No experience is ever wasted. I believe we are entrusted with the responsibility of parenthood for a reason, and it's never too late to lead our children well.

1
The Gift of Competition

Competition is Not the Enemy

If you picked up this book, chances are you care deeply about your young athlete's experience in sports, and the idea of backing off or not pushing them feels foreign, maybe even weak. You believe in hard work. You believe in competition. And you've likely sacrificed time, money, and energy to give your child every possible advantage. You don't want excuses. You want results.

Or maybe you're a parent looking for guidance, someone who wants to raise a strong, confident child through sports, and help them build the character and discipline that comes from real commitment. You want to support your child without overstepping, and to work with coaches and programs to bring out the best in your athlete and yourself.

Or maybe you're a coach, athletic director, or club sports leader searching for ways to better support your athletes by helping parents understand their role, align with your values, and contribute to something greater than wins and losses.

Whatever your role, and whatever your style, I want to start with one simple truth:

Competition is not the enemy – it's the training ground.

When guided well, competition becomes one of the most powerful tools we have to shape young athletes into strong, resilient adults by teaching grit, discipline, teamwork, and character that lasts far beyond the game.

But here's the catch: competition can be a double-edged sword.

When pushing your child turns into pressuring them, when love is measured by wins and losses, or when fear of failure drives every decision, the benefits begin to slip away. Kids can lose joy, confidence, and even their sense of purpose.

This book is about finding the middle ground

It's about learning how to push well and how to motivate and challenge young athletes without breaking their spirit. It's about helping them love the process as much as the outcome and about raising champions who win, on the scoreboard and in life.

Throughout these pages, you will learn how to:

- **Push without breaking** – Learn the difference between healthy motivation and damaging pressure.

- **Fuel passion, not fear** – Inspire effort and perseverance without sacrificing the love for the game.

- **Balance drive and well-being** – Help your child chase greatness without losing themselves in the process.

- **Show up the right way** – Navigate tough conversations, emotional moments, and sideline dynamics with clarity and confidence.

I'm not here to tell you to back off or blindly push harder. I'm here to share what I've learned as a kid raised under intense pressure, as a professional investigator trained to analyze high-stakes situations, as a coach, and as a parent raising children who are on their own sports journeys.

This book is a conversation, a bridge between the dreams we have for our kids and the reality they live every day. It's a call to action, yes, but also a call to reflection and understanding.

When Pushing Is Healthy

Some of you might worry that the message of this book is soft, overly emotional, or even anti-competition. If that's you, let me be clear right now: this book does not discourage competition. In fact, teaching competition – or a competitive spirit – when done well, is one of the greatest gifts we can give our children. It builds mental toughness, resilience, and a powerful work ethic. It teaches kids how to handle pressure, be part of a team, and push past limits. All of this comes from learning the *right kind* of competition.

The problem isn't competition itself. The problems arise when a child's identity becomes so wrapped up in winning or losing that the process of growth, joy, and learning is lost. That's when pushing becomes pressure, and healthy striving turns into harmful stress.

So how do you tell the difference? How do you push your child in a way that fuels their growth without breaking their spirit?

Pushing vs. Pressuring: Knowing the Difference

Let's draw a simple line between two types of parenting approaches:

Healthy Pushing	Harmful Pressuring
Encourages effort and growth	Demands specific results or outcomes
Respects the child's emotions	Dismisses feelings as weakness
Celebrates progress and hard work	Obsesses over winning and stats
Provides steady support and presence	Uses guilt, shame, or threats as leverage

Healthy pushing is about encouraging your child to give their best, no matter what the outcome on the scoreboard. It's showing up, even when things get hard, and praising the effort, the commitment, the hustle. Harmful pressuring is about suggesting that your child's worth is dependent on trophies, stats, or comparisons to others. It makes losing feel like failure and causes mistakes to elicit shame.

I know because I've lived on both sides. As I've explained, I grew up under constant pressure to win, and that relentless demand sharpened my competitive edge but left little room for joy. As a parent and coach, I've learned to steer away from harmful pressure and toward healthy pushing that builds the heart as well as skill.

And while I strive to be an encouraging parent, I've also learned not to chase perfection. Parenting isn't about getting it right every time, it's about a consistent, nurturing walk alongside your child that will allow them to grow and mature at their own unique pace.

Walking Alongside Your Athlete

As a parent, our role isn't to coach outcomes. It's to coach effort, attitude, and perseverance. We guide our child's habits, help them set goals, and teach them how to deal with setbacks not by avoiding them, but by facing them with courage.

Healthy pushing means:

- Setting clear, consistent expectations
- Teaching the value of follow-through on responsibilities
- Letting your child struggle sometimes, so they can grow stronger
- Recognizing when to step back so your child can take ownership

Don't misunderstand me – pushing your child to compete isn't wrong. In fact, it's necessary if you want them to develop confidence. But it only works when it's balanced with love, respect, and a focus on who your child is becoming, not just what they achieve.

At What Are You Helping Your Child Win?

We all know there's a difference between winning a game and winning in life. Sometimes, the push to win at all costs teaches lessons you don't want your child to learn, like fear of failure, comparison, or burnout. Instead, we need to help our children compete in ways that build character: integrity, perseverance, teamwork, and joy in the very act of competing.

You're not wrong for wanting your child to win. Just take care to first ask yourself what winning truly means.

Reflection Questions for Parents:

- When am I pushing my child with love, and when am I pushing out of fear or my own desires?
- What is my child learning about themselves from the way I support or pressure them?

- How can I help my child value effort and growth more than results of a competition?

Healthy competition is a powerful tool. We certainly don't want to remove the drive to compete or lower expectations. We merely want to raise the bar with wisdom and respect for the child's whole person.

2

The 1% vs. the 99%: Understanding Where Your Child Fits in Youth Sports

Let's Talk About the Elephant in the Room

There's a type of athlete we all recognize: the ultra-dedicated, single-sport kid. Maybe it's your child. The one who wakes up early to train, studies game film for fun and structures their entire life around their sport. If that's your child, I'm not here to tell you to slow them down. Keep encouraging them. Keep supporting them. Let them chase their dream.

But let's be honest, that's not most kids.

Most young athletes play because they enjoy it. They play because their friends do, because it keeps them active, because it gives them something to do. And yet, **youth sports today are often structured as if every child is, or should be, that one-in-a-hundred athlete, fully committed to a single sport, training year-round, and focused on making it to the highest level.**

And that's where we, as parents, need to pause and take a hard look at reality.

It's easy to get caught up in the culture of *more*. More training. More teams. More pressure. It's easy to believe that if your child isn't specializing, they're falling behind. Or that if they aren't pushing harder, they're missing out on future opportunities. But the truth is, most kids *aren't* wired that way. They want to play, compete, and improve, but they also want balance. They want to be kids.

It's important to keep that in mind as you read. The purpose of this book is to help you understand your child's motivations, to find the right balance between encouragement and pressure, and to ensure their sports experience serves *them*, not the other way around.

So, if your child is among the 1% chasing elite athletic goals, read with an open mind, looking for ways to better support their physical and emotional journey at the highest level. But if you reflect and realize that your child is like most – part of the 99% who play sports for growth, enjoyment, and opportunity, you will find just as much worthwhile information here as a parent of that 1%. I want to have an honest conversation about what youth sports truly offer, and how we as parents can show up with the perspective, balance, and support our kids really need.

Before you begin, please take the time to complete the Parental Involvement in Youth Sports Assessment.

This brief assessment is adapted from the **Parental Involvement in Sport Questionnaire (PISQ)** developed by Brustad (1992), a widely recognized and researched tool designed to understand how parents engage with their child's sports experience. This version is simplified for practical use while maintaining the core concepts.

How to Complete the Assessment:

Read each statement carefully and consider how it reflects your usual behavior or feelings about your child's sports participation. Be honest with yourself and select the response that best matches your typical experience:

- **Almost Never** (1) – This rarely applies to me

- **Sometimes** (2) – This applies to me occasionally

- **Often** (3) – This applies to me frequently

- **Almost Always** (4) – This is almost always true for me

Question	Almost Never (1)	Sometimes (2)	Often (3)	Always (4)
1. I encourage my child to enjoy sports for fun rather than just to win.				
2. I talk to my child about their sports performance and how they can improve.				
3. I feel proud when my child wins or performs well.				
4. I encourage my child to try their best regardless of the outcome.				
5. I sometimes feel frustrated when my child doesn't play as much as others.				
6. I attend most or all of my child's games and practices.				
7. I talk with coaches about my child's playing time and development.				
8. I expect my child to dedicate significant time to their sport.				
9. I encourage my child to participate in multiple sports or activities.				
10. I support my child's decisions about continuing or quitting their sport.				

Scoring Guide

Total your score by adding up your responses (each scored 1-4; 10 questions total). Your total will be between 10 and 40.

Score Range	Interpretation	Reflection Question
34 – 40 You consistently encourage fun, effort, and balanced involvement, fostering a positive environment for your child's growth.	**Highly Supportive** How do I continually support my child's love for the game without adding pressure?	What signs show me my child is enjoying their sports experience? How can I encourage resilience and enjoyment even when things don't go perfectly?
24 – 33 You show a good balance of encouragement and involvement but may occasionally experience frustration or place pressure on your child.	**Moderately Supportive** When do I notice feelings of frustration arise, and what triggers them?	How can I shift my focus to my child's passion rather than outcomes or expectations? Am I listening enough to how my child feels about their sports experience?
10 – 23 Your responses suggest you may sometimes feel overly invested or place higher expectations on your child's sports participation.	**Potentially Over-Involved** Am I supporting my child's wishes and autonomy in sports decisions?	How might my involvement be affecting my child's motivation or enjoyment? What steps can I take to create a more balanced pressure-free environment?

This tool is designed to encourage thoughtful reflection and promote a supportive environment for youth athletes. It is not a clinical diagnostic instrument.

Use This Information Moving Forward – The goal of this assessment is not to judge but to help you make informed, intentional decisions as you accompany your child on their sports experience.

3
Chasing Dreams

"Success is peace of mind which is a direct result of self-satisfaction in knowing you did your best to become the best you are capable of becoming."

— John Wooden, UCLA Bruins men's basketball coach, nicknamed the "Wizard of Westwood"

It started at a very early age for me. My father wanted me to be a professional baseball player, and he would do anything to help me achieve that dream. This is an all too familiar story, the *sport parent* living vicariously through their child. A parent who looks back on the athletic opportunities they didn't have or could not achieve. I have experienced this interesting phenomenon as a son, as a coach, and as a fan sitting back and watching my kids play their sport. It fascinates me how deeply involved some parents become in their child's athletic life.

As parents, we naturally dream big for our children. We picture their success in every situation, and the idea of their success becomes intoxicating, fueling an almost relentless pursuit of achievement. But in that pursuit, many parents unknowingly become the biggest obstacle to their child's growth, happiness, and long-term success in sports and yes, in life, as well.

The biggest problem I've observed is that many parents live through their child's athletic career as if it's their own or it's something they could have had. In doing so, they unintentionally chip away at the very foundation that sports are meant to build: life balance, perseverance, discipline, and character.

I believe an overbearing, unknowledgeable parent means well; after all, they want the best for their child. But I don't think they realize the degree to which they may harm their child's future. Instead of allowing their child to naturally grow into an athlete, they try to manufacture one. They become obsessive, prioritizing training over childhood, scholarships over education, and winning over everything. The result? Burned-out kids, broken family relationships and, ironically, worse athletes.

While there are countless ways a parent can unintentionally disrupt the natural and healthy development of their young athlete, three stand out as the most damaging, based on my experience:

1. Home becomes the training facility and not a home.

2. The full-ride scholarship delusion, which I call "The Golden Ticket," takes over.

3. Parents often struggle to step aside and let their child own their experience, trusting the game itself to be the teacher.

The Home Becomes a Training Facility, not a Home

Imagine a young athlete who loved baseball. At least, that's what his parents told him. He could barely remember a time when he wasn't swinging a bat, throwing a ball, or running drills in the back yard. But somewhere along the way, the game stopped feeling like a game.

When he was six, his father decided he had a future in the sport. Not just a future—**THE** future. His father, a former college player whose career had been cut short by injury, saw his son as a second chance. His mother, the organizer, mapped out his development like a CEO crafting a five-year business plan.

At first, it was fun. They built a batting cage in the back yard, then put up a small turf field, "just for practice." By the time he was eight, the barn had been converted into a full-scale training facility, complete with a weight room, sprint track, and pitching mounds. Their home became a revolving door for private trainers: hitting specialists, pitching coaches, and speed trainers.

School became secondary. Homework could be finished in the car on the way to private lessons. Friends? Only if they were teammates. Video games, movies, even simple evenings playing catch for fun were replaced by regimented drills, nutrition plans, and recovery therapy.

The young athlete learned quickly that his parents' love was tied to his performance. If he hit a home run, there were celebrations. If he struck out, silence. If he dared to say he was tired, his father would remind him, "The competition isn't sleeping, son. You want to be great, don't you?"

By twelve, the boy was exhausted. He longed to be a normal kid, to ride his skateboard through the neighborhood, to waste time with friends, to sit in his room without a schedule looming over him. But there was nowhere to escape. His home wasn't a home anymore; it was a training ground. The walls were covered in his stats, scouting reports, tournament schedules. Even family dinners turned into strategy meetings.

One night, after a grueling four-hour session with his private trainer, the boy collapsed on the turf field and just stared up at the sky. The stars blurred through his weary eyes. He could hear his parents inside, discussing his swing mechanics, oblivious to the fact that their son wasn't just losing his love for the game, he was losing himself.

He closed his eyes and whispered, "I just want to be a kid again."

But in this household, childhood wasn't part of the plan.

My own father, as I discussed earlier, approached my athletic development like a full-time job, and unfortunately, I've witnessed countless parents over the years adopting the same mentality. This relentless pursuit of success often comes at a steep cost, sacrificing everything else in the child's life.

- Vacations? Canceled, not taken, wrapped into tournament travel
- Family functions? Skipped
- Church and Youth Group? Only if there isn't a game or tournament
- School Activities? Unimportant
- Homework? Do it after the extra reps
- Friends? Only if they help with training

At such a high cost, everything revolves around making sure the child advances. Backyard batting cages are installed, garages are converted into weight rooms, and private training sessions are demanded. Instead of enjoying a childhood filled with diverse experiences, the child's life becomes an endless cycle of drills, training, and pressure. Moreover, the child is restricted from participating in any activities deemed risky or counterproductive to their specific sport, all in the name of preserving their competitive edge and maintaining peak performance.

The most troubling part of all this is that these parents genuinely believe they are doing what's best for their child, that every sacrifice, every missed family event, and every hour devoted to training is just another step toward greatness. But then comes the breaking point. One day, the child realizes they're burned out, their passion has faded, and they either walk away from the sport entirely, or worse, grow to resent the people who pushed them toward an impossible dream.

The Full-Ride Scholarship Delusion, or the "Golden Ticket"

For some parents, the unrelenting push for the golden ticket of a scholarship is their financial strategy for when their child reaches college age.

I often hear parents of young athletes envisioning their child receiving full-ride scholarships to top-tier schools. While this is completely natural, the reality is that securing a full athletic scholarship is nearly impossible these days, and college recruiters will confirm this. In fact, many student athletes end up with more academic scholarship money than athletic, proving that talent alone rarely guarantees a free ride to college.

I learned a valuable lesson years ago while spending time with John Shafer, a Territorial Scout for the San Francisco Giants in the Pacific Northwest. When I asked him about evaluating an athlete's potential, he told me, "The fastest kid in the neighborhood will always be the fastest. The kid who throws the hardest will always throw the hardest." His words hit home because they made perfect sense. While skills can be refined and some athletes will physically develop beyond expectations, there are certain innate abilities, like raw speed and arm strength, that simply can't be taught. You're either born with them, or you're not.

Here's the hard truth, whether you choose to accept it or not: **If your child has the talent to be recruited by college or professional scouts, the right opportunities will find them. If they don't have the necessary**

athletic ability, no amount of forced training, private lessons, or sacrificed childhood experiences will change that.

Let's pause here to review the healthy attributes of an athlete who will excel. Regardless of talent level, every athlete must possess a certain degree of dedication to put themselves in the best position for success. This includes working hard, being coachable, and committing to the lifestyle of an athlete: prioritizing exercise, nutrition, rest, and overall discipline. However, there is a crucial balance between being pushed in a way that fosters growth and development versus being pressured to the point of burnout or resentment. A supportive, structured environment builds strong athletes, while an overbearing approach can do just the opposite.

The Parent Who Won't Let Go

I vividly remember watching my wife coach our 8-year-old daughter's soccer team. At halftime, as she gathered the team, a father stormed over and inserted himself between the players and my wife. Without hesitation, he took over barking instructions as if he was the head coach, completely disregarding her leadership. He dictated plays, shared his own strategy, and undermined everything she had been teaching.

I once heard a college baseball coach share a frustrating story about a pitcher whose father gave him hand signals from the stands, dictating what pitches to throw. It threw the coach's entire game plan into chaos and sent the wrong message to the player, who was caught between pleasing his father and trusting his coach.

One year, while working as an assistant coach on a varsity high school baseball team, a grandparent stormed into the dugout mid-game, furious his grandson wasn't getting more playing time. Shouting and cursing, he was ready to fight the coaching staff. The scene was shocking: a grown adult disrupting a competitive game over playing time.

While writing this book, I watched my wife coach a top-level club soccer match known for producing Division I and professional players. One incredibly talented athlete stood out, with a clear path to a high-level future. But instead of shining, she was overshadowed by her father on the sideline, who was relentlessly dictating her every move. At one point, he made her stop mid-play just to look at him for instructions. The opposing team nearly scored while she was distracted. To him, none of that mattered. What mattered was executing his plan, not hers.

All of these are examples of one of the most damaging habits a parent can fall into - coaching from the sidelines. I've witnessed it at every level, from youth sports to college ball. By the time an athlete reaches college, both they and their parents should know better.

I respect the passion of parents who can't help shouting advice; it shows they care deeply about their child. Maybe you played the sport yourself, even at a higher level than the coach, and believe you know the "right" way. Maybe you question the coach's strategy. But here's the truth: good coaches have a mission and vision from the first practice to the final game. They know every player's strength, weaknesses, and tendencies, and they design a system so the team functions as one. For that to work, there must be **one voice** the athletes follow during a competition.

From the moment they're born, children are trained to listen first to their parents' voices. Second, they learn to respect authority figures: teachers, police officers, and in sports, coaches. The coach becomes the voice athletes are conditioned to follow through countless hours of practice.

Here's why that matters: if you're in a crowd of thousands and shout your child's name, they'll hear you instantly and face a split-second decision: listen to you or stay focused. That divided attention creates stress and confusion, and in sports, confusion ends up in mistakes.

When parents interrupt this system during a game, even with the best intentions, they introduce conflicting messages that distract the athlete and disrupt the team's flow. One distracted player means one position out of sync, one play broken, one opportunity lost. It's like a wolf pack hunting in silent coordination: if one wolf breaks formation or charges too soon, the prey escapes and the whole pack goes hungry.

Some parents know better but do it anyway, insisting, "You're not telling me how or when to talk to my kid." Others truly believe they're helping. But sideline coaching, no matter how well-intentioned, undermines team unity, creates unnecessary pressure, and almost always hurts performance.

If your child dreams of playing in college or professionally, one of their most valuable skills will be coachability: the ability to listen, adjust, and thrive under one leader. That starts early, with learning how to respond to the coach and succeed as part of a team. Parents play a vital role in that process when they respect the one voice guiding the team.

One team. One focus. One voice. That's how champions are made, and how championship teams are built.

Okay, so right about now you might be thinking you're the exception or that you're "just helping." But trust me, publicly questioning coaching decisions, shouting from the stands, showing up uninvited to practice, or sending late-night texts about playing time isn't helping, it's harmful. You create tension, disrupt trust, and send your child the message: *I don't believe you can handle this on your own.*

In my experience, parental overreach is far too common and persists even through college. Here are some obvious examples of crossing the line:

- Breaking down every mistake after games
- Turning car rides home into brutal film sessions
- Sideline coaching
- Confronting referees
- Fostering conflicts between private and team coaches
- Demanding positions or playing time

- Overloading training

- Encouraging playing through injuries

- Prioritizing sports over school

- Undermining team culture

- Threatening to transfer teams or schools

- Having post-game confrontations with coaches

- Becoming overinvolved in practices

- Encouraging rule-breaking

In a study by the National Alliance for Youth Sports, 70% of kids quit organized sports by the age of 13. The leading cause? Pressure from parents.

The Parent Role in Organized Sports

As parents, we play a crucial role in our child's overall success and that role is straightforward:

1. **Provide the essentials** – Ensure your child has the proper equipment and apparel to safely participate.

2. **Be their biggest fan** – Cheer for your child and their team, celebrating effort and growth over just wins and losses. Make sure you tell them often, "I love to watch you play."

3. **Support the coaching staff** – You've entrusted your most prized possession to the coaches, so back them up. Respect their decisions and allow them to do their job. Be supportive and step up when they need help. Communicate with them respectfully and privately, and seek all perspectives before challenging their decisions.

4. **Maintain perspective** – Regularly check in with your child, manage expectations about their abilities, role, and most importantly, support

them unconditionally, regardless of their role on the team.

The following National Collegiate Athletic Association (NCAA) statistics should serve as a reality check for parents, helping them set realistic expectations and understand the challenge of achieving the next level and moving on to college sports. NCAA.org is an excellent resource for both parents and athletes interested in learning more about the collegiate sports landscape.

In NCAA Division I athletics, fewer than 2% of high school athletes advance to the next level, and an even smaller percentage secure a starting position. Simply making a college roster is an enormous challenge, and the odds of reaching the professional level are even slimmer. Understanding these realities can help parents focus on what truly matters, ensuring their child enjoys the ride, develops valuable life skills, and grows as both an athlete and a person.

- **Football (Men's)**: Of the approximately 1.1 million high school football players, only about 6.5% will play at the NCAA level, and less than 1% will make it to the NFL.

- **Basketball (Men's)**: Less than 3% of high school basketball players will play at the NCAA level, and only 1.2% of NCAA athletes will make it to the NBA.

- **Basketball (Women's)**: Of the over 400,000 high school female basketball players, less than 4% will play at the NCAA level, and only 0.9% will go on to play professionally in the WNBA.

- **Baseball (Men's)**: About 7.5% of high school baseball players will go on to play at the NCAA level, and less than 10% of college players will make it to the MLB.

- **Soccer (Men's)**: Only about 6.3% of male high school soccer players will play in college, and less than 1.5% will make it to a professional league like Major League Soccer.

- **Soccer (Women's)**: Roughly 8.5% of female high school soccer players will make it to the NCAA, with less than 0.5% going on to play in professional leagues like the NWSL.

- **Volleyball (Women's)**: Around 5.5% of high school female volleyball players will play in college, and less than 1% will make it to the professional level.

- **Swimming (Men's & Women's)**: Around 6% of high school swimmers make it to the NCAA level, and less than 1% will reach the professional stage or Olympics.

- **Track & Field (Men's & Women's)**: Approximately 5.3% of high school track and field athletes compete at the NCAA level. Of those, only a fraction ever compete professionally or represent their country in international competitions like the Olympics or World Championships.

As you can see, when it comes to football, basketball, and baseball, the chances of being drafted into professional leagues are incredibly slim. Let's look at those specific stats again:

- **NFL**: Less than 1% of NCAA football players will make it to the NFL.

- **NBA**: Only about 1.2% of NCAA basketball players make it to the NBA.

- **MLB**: Of NCAA baseball players, only about 9% will make it to Major League Baseball.

So, reality check – the chances of going professional are extremely slim, but that shouldn't make the experience any less valuable.

4

The Process of Winning: Setting Healthy Expectations

The Story of Jake: A Cautionary Tale

Jake was a talented 12-year-old athlete who excelled in baseball and basketball. His parents, eager for him to succeed, pushed him to play both sports year-round. They enrolled him in select teams, private coaching, and travel leagues, believing that the more Jake played, the more likely he was to secure a college scholarship. Their expectation was clear: Jake was going to be a professional athlete, and they would stop at nothing to ensure that happened.

At first, Jake loved the games and the practice. He enjoyed being on competitive teams and relished the praise he received for his continually improving skills. But as the months wore on, something changed. The endless practices, tournaments, and constant pressure to perform began to take its toll. Jake started to dread the games. He would cry in his room before leaving for practice, not because he didn't want to play, but because he was overwhelmed by the relentless schedule and his parents' expectations. His grades started dropping, and he began withdrawing from friends and family. The joy of the sports he once loved slowly faded.

One day, after an especially difficult tournament, Jake came home and told his parents, "I don't want to play anymore." They were shocked by his sudden decision. They had invested so much time and money, and their dream of seeing him play professionally seemed to be slipping away. They didn't understand. To them, it wasn't just about their son's happiness, but about what they saw as his potential for greatness.

Jake's decision marked the beginning of a tough time for his family. The pressure to succeed had ultimately burned him out and led him to quit both of the sports he had once enjoyed. It took a long time for him to get over the emotional and mental exhaustion he'd experienced from trying to meet unrealistic expectations.

After a few weeks of reflection, Jake's parents realized they had made a mistake. They had placed so much emphasis on his future potential that they had lost sight of the importance of balance. They hadn't allowed Jake to simply be a kid. They hadn't asked themselves whether he was still enjoying the process, or whether their vision for his future was too heavy a burden for him as a twelve-year-old boy. They had been so fixated on the idea of him succeeding that they had forgotten to consider his well-being.

This story illustrates how important it is to set healthy expectations to help children not only thrive in sports but also in other aspects of their lives.

As parents, we naturally want our child to be a standout player on their team. We envision them as the captain, a starter in every game, playing every minute, making the game-winning save, catch, or shot, and being the one featured in the hometown paper with an action-packed photo capturing their heroic moment. This instinct is shared by parents of athletes at every stage, from youth leagues to elite competition, regardless of age, skill level, or team. Deep down, we ultimately want our athlete to succeed, grow, and find joy in their endeavors, especially when it comes to something as impactful as sports. When our children enter the world of organized sports, it's easy to become swept up in the excitement and pressure. We may even start to envision them playing professionally or at the highest collegiate level. But it's essential to ground those dreams in the reality of what sports are truly about.

I find it interesting that even at the highest levels of youth sports development, there is a growing movement to reframe what success means. For example, MLS NEXT, operated by Major League Soccer, is the premier boys youth soccer development league in the United States, and recently made a bold change that reflects this shift. According to a 2024 article published by *Goal.com*, the league eliminated traditional win-loss standings for players under the age of 14 and introduced a **"Quality of Play"** model to evaluate teams. Instead of focusing on final scores or rankings, this new model assesses how well players perform in key areas like passing, decision-making, movement while away from the ball, and teamwork.

The purpose behind this change is simple but powerful: to prioritize player development over results. MLS NEXT leaders recognized that putting too much emphasis on winning at a young age often leads to burnout, over-specialization, and missed opportunities for real growth. By removing the pressure of standings, the league is giving coaches and players the freedom to focus on improving skills, as well as player development and enjoyment.

For parents, this sends a clear and important message: even at the highest level of youth sports, success is no longer defined solely by the scoreboard. Growth, learning, and long-term development matter more. If the most competitive boys youth soccer league in the country is willing to deemphasize wins and losses for the sake of developing better players and healthier athletes, then surely we as parents can reframe our expectations, too.

In this chapter, we'll talk about playing sports from youth to high school and beyond, how to support athletes without applying unnecessary pressure, and the importance of recognizing their developmental stages to foster well-rounded growth. By setting healthy expectations, we can ensure that our children enjoy their time in sports and gain valuable life lessons, regardless of whether they make it to a Division I school or even go on to the pros.

The Realities of Youth Sports

Participating in sports is an excellent way for boys and girls, young men and women, to develop physical, emotional, and social skills. Organized athletics offer valuable lessons in teamwork, perseverance, leadership, and discipline. However, it's crucial for parents to understand the realities and commitments that come with immersing their child in a sport.

So, what are the realities you should prepare for when your child plays a sport from youth through high school?

- **Time commitment:** Practices, games, tournaments, and travel can consume nights and weekends, leaving little room for rest and unstructured family time.

- **Prioritizing against competing interests:** Vacation, family events, church, hobbies, other sports, and even schoolwork may at times take a back seat to the sports schedule.

- **Financial cost:** Club fees, equipment, uniforms, private lessons, and travel expenses can add up quickly, especially in competitive programs.

- **Emotional highs and lows:** Your child may face frustration, failure, success, and pressure, all of which can be in the same week. Learning to cope with the emotional roller coaster comes with the territory.

- **Physical demands and injury risk:** Sports push the body, and while that builds strength, it also brings the possibility of acute and overuse injuries, or even burnout if not properly managed.

- **Social impact:** Sports tend to shape your child's social world. Coaches, teammates, and competition can impact confidence, friendships, and identity.

- **Not everyone is the star:** Your child may need to embrace a role outside of the spotlight. Learning to serve the team in any capacity is valuable but can be hard for a child to accept.

Two critical factors that parents and athletes often must manage in youth sports are the benefits of being a multi-sport athlete and the increasing pressure to specialize in a single sport.

Multi-Sport Athlete

I am a strong proponent of **multi-sport participation**, especially among younger athletes. In my experience, athletes who rotate through seasonal sports tend to develop in a more well-rounded, balanced, and healthier way than those who focus on just one sport year-round.

Recent studies and expert recommendations from sources such as *Athletes Untapped, BSN Sports, and Kidsports.org* point to the significant benefits of youth athletes participating in multiple sports. According to a summary of data compiled by these sources, multi-sport athletes are less likely to suffer from overuse injuries, burnout or drop out of sports altogether. Playing multiple sports exposes young people to a broader range of movement patterns, motor skills, and physical challenges, which promotes more complete athletic development and reduces repetitive stress on specific joints and muscle groups. It also enhances mental agility, as kids are required to adapt to different strategies, teammates, and coaching styles. This variety not only keeps sports fresh and enjoyable, but it also helps young athletes develop leadership, communication, and resilience.

In fact, many of today's top college and professional athletes grew up as multi-sport athletes, and research conducted by Rugg, Kadoor, Feeley, and Pandya (2021) in the *Orthopaedic Journal of Sports Medicine* has shown that the vast majority of NCAA Division I athletes and over 90% of first-round NFL draft picks did not specialize early in a single sport. Instead, they benefited from the diverse physical and mental foundation that multi-sport participation provides. While early specialization may appear to offer a competitive edge, it often comes at the cost of long-term development, overall well-being, and a sustained love for the game of whichever sport they're playing.

Of course, being a multi-sport athlete **does not mean being everything to everyone** or committing to multiple teams simultaneously in the same season. When young athletes are torn between team obligations, it can undermine one of the most important life lessons sports offers: **commitment.**

Here are a couple of examples:

- I once coached a high school junior who was an exceptional player and clearly the top player on our varsity team. This athlete was actively being recruited by several top-tier college programs. During the season, this player requested permission to miss one or two practices a week with our high school team in order to train with their club team instead.

On the surface, it may have made some sense. The player would likely receive quality instruction with the benefit of individual coaching and development opportunities with the club team. From a performance standpoint, their skills wouldn't have suffered. But the issue wasn't about talent or training. It was about commitment to our team.

Allowing them to operate on a different schedule would have sent a message to the whole team. It would have signaled that being part of the high school program was optional, that showing up consistently didn't matter, and that individual pursuits outweighed collective responsibility. In the end, this wavering commitment didn't just hurt the player's ability to lead and connect with teammates but also disrupted the cohesion and culture of the entire program. From the beginning of the varsity season, our team policy was clear: one missed practice, unless due to illness or a school activity and the result would be having to sit out a full game. It was a simple one-for-one policy. Given the choice, the player ultimately chose to forgo the club practice and remain fully committed to the high school team, which I believe was the right choice.

- While coaching a high school-aged club baseball team, I received a message one evening from one of my players. He told me he wasn't feeling well and wouldn't be able to make it to practice. His teammates were frustrated, not just because he was gone, but because they knew exactly where he was. He was playing in a summer league basketball game organized by the high school's basketball coach. The kicker? The gym he was playing in was on the same campus and less than 100 yards from our baseball field!

Coming from a law enforcement background, I've always followed the mantra: *"Don't believe what you hear, believe half of what you see, and verify everything."* So, I walked into the gym during practice, and there he was, my starting third baseman and the number two hitter in the lineup, running up and down the court. My first thought was, *He sure doesn't look sick to me.* I later had a discussion with him about commitment and the impression his actions had left on his teammates, who had shown up and honored their shared responsibility.

Commitment is more than showing up. It's about **respecting your team, your role, and the effort everyone else is putting in.** When athletes fail to commit, it forces coaches into tough decisions regarding playing time and leadership roles, which often favor those who consistently show dedication and reliability. This isn't about punishing kids; it's about reinforcing the traits that build strong teammates and, eventually, successful adults.

Most of us know that **commitment is a critical skill in life**.

The Specialization and Comparison Challenge

If you're a parent of a young athlete, you've probably felt it - that knot in your stomach when you see other kids training year-round, playing for elite clubs, and already locking into one sport or one position. You scroll past the highlight reels on social media, hear other parents comparing tournament schedules, private coaches, and specialized gear, and you can't help but wonder: *Are we doing enough?* It's not jealousy. It's not even ambition run wild. It's the simple nagging fear of watching your child fall behind in a race you're not even sure they should be running.

But remember, there is a hidden cost to narrowing a child's athletic focus too early. Today, young athletes face immense pressure to choose one sport, sometimes even a single position, before they've had the chance to explore their full potential. While early specialization is often promoted as the fast track to success, research and real-world experience tell a more complicated story.

Focusing too narrowly at a young age can hinder a child's overall athletic development and significantly increase the risk of burnout and overuse injuries. Research published in the *Clinical Journal of Sports Medicine* suggests these account for nearly half of all youth sports injuries. The constant push to succeed, win, and specialize can overshadow the true purpose of sports, which should be fun, growth, and the development of life skills.

I've seen many parents wrestle with the same questions: *When should my child join a serious club team? Is it better to play multiple sports or go all-in on one? Will they fall behind if we don't keep pace with everyone else?* The fear is real. Skip offseason club play and your child might lose ground to peers. But in all my years, I have yet to meet an athlete who reached the college Division I or professional level solely because they specialized early. More often, the most successful athletes had parents who helped them balance sports with other life commitments, giving them time to develop naturally.

Research backs this up. Dr. Jean Côté, a leading sports psychologist, found that specializing before age 12 raises the risk of burnout and injury. The National Federation of State High School Associations reports that only 7.4% of U.S. high school athletes go on to play at the NCAA level, and a *Journal of Sports Sciences* study estimates that less than 1% make it to professional ranks. So once again, it's clear from the data that the odds of turning pro are slim. The lessons from sports, however, are invaluable: accountability, time management, teamwork, perseverance, resilience, and mental toughness.

I've met families caught in the tug-of-war of what can feel like a make-or-break decision. One father told me about the top program in his region, which called for three to four practices a week, requiring a 90-minute drive each way. The training would be elite, but the cost was steep: weekends gone, family time lost, and a budget stretched to the breaking point.

On the flip side, I've seen parents whose children started later, like the father whose son began baseball at twelve, only to realize most teammates had been sharpening their skills for years. The boy loved the sport, but the gap in experience was impossible to ignore.

The truth is, there is an advantage to starting early and training consistently. A young athlete with more reps under their belt will likely reach a higher level sooner. But there is also a physical, emotional, and financial cost that can quietly erode both a child's love for the game and the family's well-being.

The challenge for parents isn't to mimic what everyone else is doing, but to make intentional, values-based decisions for their own child's unique path. Comparison will always tempt you to measure progress against the so-called "pipeline kids," but what your child truly needs is not just more hours on the field, but a well-designed thoughtful plan that balances growth, passion, and overall well-being.

If you're wrestling with these questions right now, you're not alone. Many families have walked this road, and while the answer isn't always obvious or straightforward, the right conversation can bring clarity, confidence, and a plan that works for both your child and your family.

Before you commit to the next season, pause for a moment. Step back from the noise, the pressure, and the comparisons. Ask yourself what kind of athlete and person you want your child to become. And remember, there are people who've walked this very same path before. This is the time when seeking advice from those who have been through the ups and downs can make all the difference. Their perspective might be the thing that helps you see the next step more clearly. Whether it's through trusted mentors, experienced coaches, or resources like Raising Champions Media, support is available to help you through this important season.

The Natural Rhythm of Sports – Staying Steady Through Peaks and Valleys

The ups and downs of sports are not setbacks; they're rehearsals for life. Every athlete will face the emotional highs of victory and the sting of defeat, the physical demands of training, and the mental strain of competition. These moments, while challenging, are among the greatest life-training opportunities a young person can experience. When guided by someone who understands how to bring steady calm in turbulent moments, a young athlete learns how to positively adapt in a dynamic environment and how to become resilient in times of struggle, both of which are skills that will carry far beyond the field. After all, doesn't every career, every workplace, and every life path have its own wins and losses? Helping a young athlete handle the roller coaster of a season is, in many ways, preparing them to thrive in the unpredictable game of life.

As a young athlete, I found myself under a lot of pressure trying to perform well in front of professional scouts and college recruiters. I remember the Giants scout noticing my struggles and offering me a simple but powerful insight. To this day, I can still hear his voice: "It's all about peaks and valleys." He explained that every athlete experiences moments when everything seems to click. Those are the peaks. And every athlete also goes through times when nothing goes right. Those are the valleys. But becoming stuck on either side for too long means you risk losing your way. The key, he told me, is learning to find your way back to the middle.

This mindset became a consistent thread in how I coached and raised my kids in sports. I made sure every player I coached, and my own kids, understood that **the peaks and valleys of participating in sports are normal and part of the natural rhythm of any practice and game performance,** regardless of talent level or position. I also emphasized this during every preseason parent meeting. It was important to me that the perspective parents bring to the field, and their expectations, were grounded. Living too much on the highs or lows can negatively affect the entire team. The real challenge for players and parents alike is learning how to deal with those moments without getting lost and finding a steady path that fuels growth and confidence. For an athlete, the goal is to find their *set point*, the mental and emotional middle ground where they can compete with focus and perspective, regardless of performance, wins, and loses. This even-keeled approach fosters resilience. For a parent, the goal should be the same.

Here's where it gets tricky: parents and players can be on completely different emotional tracks, not only between games but in the moments during a game. A player might be riding a peak, feeling confident, focused, and performing well, while the parent is frustrated from an earlier mistake or external stress unrelated to the current game. Conversely, a parent might be emotionally high or low based on the player's current performance, riding those ups and downs right alongside them. This emotional roller coaster from parents reacting to each play, call, or score can create a volatile sideline environment. When a player is doing well, an overly exuberant parent might unintentionally add pressure or distract the athlete by amplifying expectations. When a player is struggling, a parent's visible disappointment or anxiety can deepen the player's frustration or self-doubt.

These mixed emotional currents, especially when parents ride their own highs and lows during the game, can cloud a player's focus and disrupt their ability to find balance and perform at their best. Players are often closely watching their parents and the parent group, so they're picking up on their emotions. When they sense tension, frustration, or negativity, it sends a signal that the post-game interaction (for example, the car ride home) might be stressful or filled with difficult questions. This anticipation can amplify a player's anxiety, adding pressure long before the game is even over.

This disconnect becomes especially apparent during games, when parental emotions tend to run high. Whether it's frustration over a referee's call, the game score, or a coach's decision, parents' visible emotional reactions send powerful signals, not only to their own child but to the entire sideline environment. Game officials, like referees and umpires, are trained to observe this sideline behavior; repeated displays of negative or confrontational emotions from parents can lead to warnings, penalties, or even ejections. Beyond disciplinary consequences, this charged energy shapes the emotional atmosphere of the game. It can unknowingly push the athlete or entire team into a valley of distraction, anxiety, or tension, disrupting focus and flow. On the other hand, positive, steady support from parents can elevate the team's collective energy, helping players find their peak performance state.

Understanding this dynamic is critical. The sideline is more than just a place to watch the game. It's a living emotional ecosystem, much like a symphony, where every note and every emotion affects the harmony of the whole. Parents who maintain an even-keeled presence, despite highs and lows, model resilience and emotional control that athletes learn to mirror. This consistency helps athletes manage their own peaks and valleys with greater confidence and composure, ultimately fostering growth and success both on and off the field. Like any great symphony, success depends on a steady beat and a unified sound, and when everyone plays in harmony, the performance is impressive.

Research confirms that the emotional tone on the sidelines, whether positive, negative, or neutral, significantly impacts youth athletes' stress, motivation, and enjoyment. A study of 67 teenage athletes found that positive parental behavior during games, such as cheering and encouragement, led to better sportsmanship and enjoyment, while negative behaviors like yelling or criticizing led to antisocial conduct and decreased enjoyment (Crozier, 2024). A broader systematic review echoed these findings, showing that excessive parental involvement often increases an athlete's stress and reduces motivation, whereas parent actions grounded in understanding, praise, and autonomy bolster enjoyment and intrinsic motivation (Smith et al., 2021). Additionally, resources like the *Sport Parent Guide* highlight the real-world impact of verbal sideline behaviors, which reinforce that consistent, calm, and supportive energy is foundational to fostering an environment where young athletes can grow with focus and resilience (Dorsch, Smith, Wilson, & McDonough, 2015).

Parents and coaches can set healthy expectations at the start of a season by making one principle clear: **We don't get too high, and we don't get too low. We focus on effort, growth, and learning.** Celebrate the good moments, yes, but with perspective. Support through the bad moments, but with steadiness. This kind of consistency is what gives young athletes the freedom to grow without fear of emotional whiplash from the people they trust most.

Avoiding Pressure: How to Help Your Athlete Enjoy the Game

As a coach, I often encouraged players to "win everything," whether it was a relay race at the end of practice or something as simple as being the first to tie their shoes before the race. I believed that even in the smallest tasks, like tying shoes before a race, the mindset of striving to win could set the tone for bigger challenges ahead. I aimed to create a culture of competition and a winning mindset. I believe this approach to coaching instills discipline, focus, and a drive for success, which can only be beneficial for players.

But it's equally important to teach athletes how to persevere through failure in a constructive way, and that coaches should guide that process. As much as we coaches love to see our athletes succeed, there's a fine line between encouragement and excessive pressure. Some of you may disagree, but I believe that good coaches (with proper oversight) should be the only ones responsible for mentally and physically pushing athletes, regardless of age or level. After all, coaches are entrusted by both players and parents to do just this, and when done right, they should be able to push them to their best effort without breaking their spirit.

At any given sporting event, everyone has a role to play. The athlete's job is to compete, the coach's role is to lead and develop the players, the official ensures the game is played fairly, and the parent's role is to be a supportive fan. The parent is not the coach, the coach is not the official, and the player is not in charge. But too often, parents blur these lines, placing undue pressure on their children. Ambition and encouragement are valuable, of course, but we parents must allow our children the space to grow, develop, and, most importantly, enjoy the game.

Overstepping these boundaries can create unnecessary stress for the athlete, interfere with the coach's ability to lead, and disrupt the integrity of the game. We parents need to remind ourselves that our role is to support, not to direct or influence the outcomes of the game.

By respecting these roles, we help create a positive environment where young athletes can thrive.

Understanding roles and responsibilities within youth and high school sports is essential for fostering a positive and effective team dynamic. The chart below outlines the key roles in any sport: coaches, players, parents, and support staff, as well as how they interact to ensure the success of the team. By clarifying these roles, we can promote better communication, collaboration, and a shared commitment to the development of young athletes. I think this chart is a valuable tool to show us exactly how everyone contributes to the success of the team in their own role.

TEAM ROLES AND RESPONSIBILITIES	
PARENT	• Offers Physical and Emotional Support • Is a Positive and Supportive Fan • Encourages Self-Control and Realism • Trusts and Partners with Coaches
COACH	• Provides Leadership and Development • Teaches Skills and Tactics • Builds Relationships and Trust
OFFICIAL	• Enforces Rules • Ensures Fairness
PLAYER	• Is Coachable and Has a Growth Mindset • Is Team-Oriented • Takes Ownership of Effort and Attitude • Competes

To help your athlete enjoy sports and develop a healthy relationship with physical activity, it's crucial to focus on their well-being, both mentally and physically. I've seen athletes perform better when they're free from the fear of failure, regardless of age. Mistakes should always be okay, and the idea that they're not only hinders growth and the child's love or passion for the game. Based on my years of experience, I believe the focus should be on effort and enjoyment until around age 12 or 13, with minimal emphasis on winning. Of course, it's also true that every athlete, no matter how old they are, wants to win. Every child knows the difference between winning and losing, and the point of the game is to win. So, while focusing on effort should be a priority, it's obviously not the complete picture. As athletes mature, winning becomes even more important to them, so learning to channel their effort into the process of winning is essential. Ultimately, true enjoyment of the game comes from being able to showcase the effort and growth that leads to victory.

Understanding Developmental Stages and Supporting Growth

It's always fascinating to watch young players dominate at the 10- to 12-year-old level. For instance, you might see a 12-year-old boy with the beginning of a mustache and a deepening voice hitting home runs effortlessly, leaving everyone in awe. His peers might think he's the next Babe Ruth. But here's the thing: when that boy turns 13, the game changes. The field becomes larger, and the other players catch up in size and strength. Suddenly, he can no longer rely on his physical advantages alone. Without the skills to match, that player often fades into the background.

This is a reminder that **physical maturity alone won't carry an athlete**. Growth, skill development, and adaptability are key. As most of us know, young athletes mature at different rates, and their abilities will shift over time as they grow physically, mentally, and emotionally.

I think U.S. Soccer gets it right when it comes to the big-picture development of young athletes. They understand that growth isn't just about age, but about **biological maturity** and the **emotional and cognitive readiness** that comes with it. In their *bio-banding initiative* video on YouTube, they illustrate this beautifully: rather than grouping kids strictly by birth year, teams are formed based on where players are in their physical development. This allows later-maturing athletes to compete in more developmentally appropriate environments, fostering confidence and belonging, which helps children find joy in the process, not just in winning. It's a model that mirrors how elite coaches nurture long-term success by prioritizing growth curves over short-term results.

It's valuable for parents **to see the whole field** and celebrate incremental progress and emotional maturity throughout their child's athletic career. Understanding the developmental stages of their young athletes can help support growth without pushing them beyond their current abilities.

According to Dr. Thomas Best, a professor of sports medicine at Ohio State University, children's bodies undergo significant physical changes from the ages of 6 to 18. These changes naturally impact their performance in sports. Dr. Best explains that during early childhood, the focus should be on general physical activity and motor skill development, while late adolescence is often when children can begin to specialize and focus on one sport.

The American Academy of Pediatrics further explains that the development of fundamental motor skills (such as running, jumping, and throwing) is most critical in the early years. It's not until children reach the ages 12-14 that they may begin to experience the specialized physical and mental demands of competitive sports.

As our kids enter their teenage years, their focus may shift more toward competition, but we must remember to also nurture their emotional and psychological growth. Dr. John Heil, a leading sports psychologist, points out that mental skills like resilience, self-confidence, and emotional regulation are just as vital as physical talent when it comes to success in sports. Supporting your child's emotional health by encouraging a positive mindset, managing stress, and fostering a love for the sport is just as important as their physical training.

Understanding the timeline of physical, emotional, and psychological growth will help you figure out when to encourage your child to push harder, when to give them room to breathe, and when to step back and let them grow at their own pace.

Conclusion: Establishing a Healthy Perspective

The bottom line is that youth sports is about more than just winning or achieving the highest levels of competition. As parents, it's natural to want to see our children succeed and excel, but it's essential to remind ourselves of the true value of sports: the life lessons they teach, the development of physical and mental skills, and the joy that comes from participating and growing.

While the pressure to specialize early and perform at an elite level can be overwhelming, we must allow our children the time and space to develop their skills across multiple sports and understand that their worth isn't solely defined by their performance on the field. By focusing on effort, enjoyment, and the process of learning, we can foster an environment where athletes thrive emotionally, mentally, and physically. Ultimately, supporting our children means balancing ambition with healthy expectations, ensuring that they not only succeed but also enjoy the experience and grow into well-rounded individuals, no matter where their athletic path may lead.

5

Fostering a Love for the Game

Can parents take a page from the playbooks of legendary coaches to inspire their kids to love the sport while staying competitive?

UCLA basketball coach John Wooden once said, "A good coach can change a game. A great coach can change a life." Wooden's coaching philosophy reflects that a coach is far more than just a teacher of skills and plays. They are a mentor who inspires growth beyond the game. They model character and integrity, showing athletes how to win with grace and lose with dignity. A great coach understands the unique needs of each athlete in their care and fosters a team environment rooted in trust and respect. Ultimately, the role of a coach extends far beyond the field, shaping not only players but the people they become.

The following legendary coaches exemplify the power of fostering player enjoyment while maintaining the necessary competitiveness to achieve success. They have all built their legacies not just by winning, but by creating environments where athletes felt supported, valued, and inspired to fall in love with the game. Their philosophies are a powerful reminder of the importance of balancing competition with the joy of playing.

John Wooden (UCLA Basketball Coach)

One of the most successful coaches in NCAA basketball history, Wooden built his success on the foundation of player enjoyment and mental well-being. His "Pyramid of Success" emphasized not just physical excellence, but also traits like enthusiasm, cooperation, and poise. He always stressed the importance of loving the game, telling his players, "Success is peace of mind, which is a direct result of self-satisfaction in knowing you did your best to become the best you are capable of becoming." (Wooden & Jamison, 2005). His ability to create a positive atmosphere that made players enjoy the game while striving for excellence helped him lead UCLA to 10 NCAA titles in 12 years.

Clive Charles (University of Portland Soccer Coach)

Charles was a beloved figure in American soccer, known for his passionate commitment to developing not only skilled players but also good people. As head coach at the University of Portland, he fostered a culture of joy and respect for the game, encouraging his athletes to play with creativity and heart. His coaching extended beyond tactics; he emphasized character, teamwork, and a lifelong love for soccer. Many of his players and colleagues remember him for his mentorship and the uplifting environment he cultivated, which helped shape the growth of soccer on the West Coast and in the United States (Charles, 2003).

Tony Dungy (NFL Coach, Former High School Coach)

Before becoming a legendary NFL coach, Tony Dungy was known for fostering a culture of respect and enjoyment of the game. He often spoke about the importance of developing players not just as athletes, but as people. Dungy's coaching philosophy focused on creating positive relationships and having fun while competing. He believed in creating a family-like atmosphere, where players felt comfortable and valued. His emphasis on mental well-being and teaching the game with integrity helped him lead the Indianapolis Colts to a Super Bowl victory in 2007 (Dungy, 2007).

Pat Summitt (University of Tennessee Women's Basketball Coach)

Summitt was one of the greatest women's basketball coaches in history, known for her ability to motivate and inspire her players while fostering a love for the game. She emphasized a culture of discipline and respect but also stressed the importance of enjoying the game and playing with passion. Her coaching style, which combined tough love with emotional intelligence, led her to win 1,098 games and build a powerhouse program at Tennessee. Her legacy is a testament to the value of creating an environment where athletes love what they do and are driven by purpose (Summitt & Andrews, 2010).

Mike Krzyzewski (Duke University Basketball Coach)

Coach K, one of the most successful and respected coaches in college basketball history, built a legacy of success by blending competitiveness with emotional intelligence. Krzyzewski emphasized the importance of enjoying the game and building relationships with his players, which helped them thrive both on and off the court. His holistic approach to coaching combined discipline with personal development, and he guided Duke University to five NCAA championships. His philosophy encouraged players to embrace the process, not just the outcomes, and to stay connected to the joy that the game brings (Krzyzewski, 2013).

Tara VanDerveer (Stanford Women's Basketball Coach)

VanDerveer is one of the winningest coaches in NCAA history and a Hall of Famer who embodies the balance of competitiveness and joy. She has consistently built her Stanford program on respect, teamwork, and love for the game, while mentoring athletes who go on to succeed in life beyond basketball. Her philosophy emphasizes not just championships (she has three NCAA titles) but also creating an environment where athletes enjoy the process of learning and improving. She has often spoken about helping players "play with joy" and focus on being the best version of themselves, both as athletes and people (Wikipedia 2025; Associated Press 2024).

Jim Valvano (North Carolina State Men's Basketball Coach)

Valvano led North Carolina State to a national championship in 1983 and was known for his ability to make basketball fun while demanding the best from every player. He famously said, "My father gave me the greatest gift anyone could give another person, he believed in me." Valvano's coaching philosophy centered around belief in his players, creating a fun, supportive atmosphere, and instilling in them the desire to be their best. His teams played with joy and energy, and he was known for motivating his players through positive reinforcement. (Valvano, 1993).

Nick Saban Jr. (University of Alabama Football)

Saban is one of the most successful football coaches in college history. He knew that love for the game was critical to long-term success, and has said that his approach to coaching involved developing players who had a passion for their craft and a desire to improve continuously. He encouraged his athletes to embrace the process and the fundamentals of football rather than just focusing on championships. By creating a competitive yet supportive environment, he ensured his players remained focused on enjoying the game while constantly improving. His leadership allowed players to embrace both the challenges and rewards of football, while keeping their passion for the game alive even through adversity (Saban, 2015).

Jürgen Klopp (Liverpool FC, Premier League Soccer)

Klopp, who retired in 2024, was known for his energetic and engaging coaching style, and brought a sense of joy and excitement to Liverpool FC. His teams were known for their high pressing, attacking football, and Klopp's infectious enthusiasm and passion for the game were contagious to his players. He cultivated an environment where his players could express themselves freely on the pitch, knowing that mistakes are part of the process. He encouraged them to enjoy the game, take risks, and play with confidence. Klopp's emphasis on team spirit, fun, and passion for football helped Liverpool become one of the most successful teams in Europe, with players consistently expressing their love for the game under his guidance (Klopp, 2020).

Of course, these examples represent just a small sample of the many great coaches dedicated to fostering a love for the game. There are countless others who prioritize player development and create environments where young athletes can grow, learn, and discover their passion for sport. This should encourage parents to actively support their child in whatever sport(s) they choose, helping them develop skills, build confidence, and find their own path in a game they genuinely enjoy.

Shared themes from these coaching philosophies:

- **Emphasis on Enjoyment and Love for the Game**

  All of the coaches named above highlighted the importance of fostering a love for sport and creating an environment where athletes enjoy playing. This is key in helping athletes perform at their best, since enjoyment leads to passion and commitment. When we put pressure on our children to excel or focus too much on winning, it can stifle this enjoyment and potentially lead to burnout.

Focus on Mental Well-being and Personal Growth

These coaches know that success in sports is not just about physical ability but also about mental health and personal development. They prioritized building confidence, resilience, and a healthy mindset in their players, which helped them handle both failures and successes. We parents need to step back and let coaches guide their child's growth, both as athletes and as individuals, rather than imposing external pressures on our kids.

- Encouraging Process Over Outcome

  Whether it's Wooden's "Pyramid of Success," Dungy's emphasis on relationships, or Klopp's focus on enjoying the process, these coaches all stressed the importance of enjoying the journey rather than obsessing over outcomes like wins or championships. From these lessons, parents can learn to help their children focus on learning, effort, and growth, rather than demanding immediate results. This approach cultivates a love for the game and a sustainable passion that leads to long-term success.

In this chapter, we will explore how to encourage this enjoyment, how to balance the fun with commitment, and how positive reinforcement can help build a lasting love for the game. If we can teach our children to love the game itself, rather than just the outcomes, we will be laying the foundation for a lifelong passion for physical activity, competition, and personal achievement.

Encouraging Enjoyment: The Heart of Sports

From the first time a child tosses a football, throws a baseball, dribbles a basketball, or kicks a soccer ball across a field, the end goal should be fun and enjoyment.

According to Dr. Jean Cote, a leading sports psychologist, **"Sports should first and foremost be a source of joy, not stress."** It's easy to lose sight of this amidst the pressures of competition, but research (and common sense!) shows that children are more likely to remain active and involved in sports when they're having fun.

A study by the National Institute of Health found that kids who enjoy sports are more likely to stick with them through their teenage years, leading to a lifetime of physical activity and improved health outcomes.

To encourage enjoyment, it's important to keep the pressure low and focus on fostering a love for the game itself. This might mean playing games outside of organized practice, celebrating small victories along the way, and providing plenty of opportunities for unstructured play. Allowing your child to explore and play without the added weight of performance expectations can nurture that deep-rooted love for the game.

Balancing Fun and Commitment: The Importance of Recognizing Athletics as a Journey

The Story of Jason: Purpose that grew with the game

From the moment Jason laced up his first pair of cleats at age 6, he was hooked on soccer. The fields were his playground; the ball was his closest companion. There was no pressure, no expectation beyond the pure joy of running, kicking, and laughing with his friends. It wasn't about winning or losing, but about playing the game he loved. His supportive parents let him experience every aspect of the game without pushing for more than he could handle.

As Jason grew, so did his skills. By middle school, he began to realize that he wasn't just good at soccer; he was very good. He loved the challenge of a close match, the satisfaction of a perfectly executed pass, and the thrill of scoring a goal. But something began to change. Practices became more intense. Coaches began to talk about "what it takes" to play at a higher level. Soon, more structure, a greater focus on technique, and a commitment to fitness were being demanded of Jason.

He felt the shift. Gone were the carefree days of running just because it was fun. Now, there were drills, fitness tests, and expectations. His parents still cheered him on from the sidelines, but they noticed the change too. Jason's pure love of the game was still there, but now it was mixed with something more serious. Jason had started to realize that this game could take him somewhere if he fully committed himself to it.

High school brought a new level of competition. As a sophomore, Jason earned a spot on the varsity team, and suddenly, his personal success was intertwined with his team's success. He no longer played just for the joy of the game; he played for the team, for the coach, and for every single person who relied on him. At first, the pressure felt overwhelming. There were moments when he wanted to go back to the days when all that mattered was kicking the ball around with his friends and having fun. But he knew that playing at a high level demanded something more from him: accountability.

It was no longer just about showing up to practice. It was about working every day to improve his skills, pushing through the exhaustion, and being a reliable teammate. The mental and physical demands of the sport were greater than ever, but Jason learned to manage them. He became more disciplined, setting aside time for individual training, working on his weaknesses, and learning to communicate with his teammates in ways he had never done before.

The summer before his senior year, Jason played in a high-stakes tournament that would give him the opportunity to showcase his talents to college scouts. His team didn't win, but Jason's performance was enough to get the attention of several college coaches. He had arrived.

Today, as a freshman in college, Jason plays for a competitive Division I soccer team. He still loves the game, but his love is more nuanced now. He's no longer just playing for fun—he's playing for his future, his teammates, and the legacy of those who believed in him along the way. He knows that while talent got him this far, it's the hard work, discipline, and accountability that will get him to the next level. What he once thought was a simple game has now become a test of endurance, character, and resilience.

As he reflects on how he made it this far, Jason recognizes the beauty in the slow, steady growth he experienced. From the carefree joy of kicking a ball around at 6 years old to the structured, often intense practices of a college athlete, he's learned the importance of loving the game, but also the value of growing at a pace that honors the demands of the passion and commitment he feels. He understands that hard work doesn't detract from the joy—it enhances it. He's also discovered that being accountable to his team and understanding the role he plays in their success is just as important as any individual accolades.

Jason has come to understand that success isn't just about winning games or earning scholarships; it's about the journey. The discipline learned over the years, the accountability called for in a team environment, and the growth, not just as an athlete but as a person - all these are core elements of his success. He's realized that while the love of the game started as a spark, it's the hard work, the relationships, and the lessons learned along the way that turned it into a lifelong passion.

As children move into their teenage years and beyond, the need for greater commitment and hard work becomes a natural part of their athletic development. During this stage, they need to start taking their sport more seriously and embrace the discipline required to excel. Striking a balance between enjoying the game and dedicating themselves to improving their skills, developing their game IQ, and growing as a valuable team member will make all the difference in their experience.

Dr. Michael Gervais is a renowned sports psychologist who works with elite athletes. He explains that the path to mastery in any discipline (including sports) depends on both deep commitment and a genuine love for the process. But the commitment must never outweigh the joy. If the joy starts to diminish, then the risk of burnout and disengagement increases. The ability to have fun while being committed to improving is what keeps athletes motivated.

As I'm sure we all know, sports should not be a chore or something that feels forced. It's important for both parents and coaches to create an environment where children feel supported, challenged, and most importantly, are enjoying themselves. This balance can be achieved by ensuring our children have moments for rest, reflection, and casual play, but that they also understand the value of hard work, practice, and dedication to improvement.

The Power of Positive Reinforcement: Praising Effort Over Results

One of the most powerful tools parents can use to cultivate a lasting love for the game is **positive reinforcement.** Praising effort over results will help children develop a growth mindset, where they understand that effort, learning, and perseverance lead to progress and success, more so than just innate talent or final scores.

Dr. Carol Dweck, a psychologist and researcher at Stanford University, has found that when children are praised for their effort rather than their inherent abilities, they are more likely to embrace challenges, persist through setbacks, and grow into resilient, confident individuals. She explains that **"A growth mindset—the belief that skills and abilities can be developed through hard work and dedication, is crucial for long-term success."**

When we focus on praising our child's effort, we are reinforcing the idea that success comes from hard work, not from perfection. Instead of focusing solely on the scoreboard, let's celebrate things like teamwork, trying new techniques, and perseverance through tough moments. By making effort the centerpiece of our encouragement, we are helping our children see the value in the process, not just the outcome.

In my opinion, helping our children develop a strong growth mindset is one of the most valuable things we can do for their personal and athletic development. In the world of sports, when a child learns to embrace and apply a growth mindset, they become more coachable, accountable as a teammate, and take full responsibility for their actions and growth as an athlete. Frankly, a growth mindset opens the door to progress in every situation.

When an athlete has a healthy growth mindset, they become more coachable and will:

- **Receive Feedback Positively**: They are able to take in feedback from various sources without feeling offended or criticized. The truth is, any athlete unable to receive constructive criticism will not grow. Embracing feedback leads to improvement and progress.

- **Bounce Back from Challenges**: They develop resilience, meaning they can quickly bounce back from setbacks. One common trait among successful athletes, and successful individuals, for that matter, is the ability to swiftly recover from adversity.

- **Adapt**: Great athletes are flexible and can adjust to new situations, new environments, or new needs. They can pivot when needed and thrive in ever-changing circumstances, which is fundamental to long-term success.

- **Pursue Consistent Improvement**: With a growth mindset, an athlete will always seek to improve, never settling for mediocrity. They understand that growth needs to be continuous, not a one-time event, and they are driven to keep progressing.

- **Develop Self-Awareness**: They are self-reflective, seeking to understand their strengths and weaknesses. A growth mindset encourages athletes to have a forward-looking game IQ, where they embrace difficult conversations and confront challenges head-on. This awareness not only improves their performance but contributes to their overall development as a player and as a person.

Encouraging your athletes to develop a growth mindset will not only help them improve on the field but will lay the foundation for success in life beyond sports. This way of thinking is a powerful tool that promotes an environment where progress, resilience, and accountability are at the forefront of personal and athletic growth.

Addressing a Specific Group of Athletes

I want to take a moment to address a specific group of athletes: those who have reached an elite level in their particular sport.

During my high school years, I was fortunate to be recognized as one of the top baseball players in the country. This recognition opened doors for me to play on several elite teams, sometimes as a pick-up player, other times as a full-time rostered player. Because of my skill level, I often had the opportunity to step into different roles, sometimes taking over a starting position, other times filling in for someone else in the lineup.

At first glance, it might seem like I had the ability to get whatever I wanted on the field, but the reality was more complex. Every opportunity I was given came with a responsibility - an expectation to perform and constantly earn my place. It would have been easy to settle into a mindset of entitlement, to expect more because I had earned my spot, but I quickly realized that true success came from something greater: a continual commitment to growth, no matter what the circumstances.

Being placed in different roles wasn't just about playing time. It was a golden opportunity for me to improve. I could have seen each new situation as a challenge to my comfort zone, but instead, I saw it as a chance to improve, to adjust, and to learn. I focused not on what I thought I deserved, but on how I could grow.

This mindset wasn't just important for me; it was important for my parents, as well. They had to adopt the same mentality, recognizing that the path to success isn't always about securing the "right" spot, but about embracing and trusting the process.

To the parents reading this: No matter where your child stands on the team, whether they're a starter, a role player, or fighting for time on the field, **YOU** have a powerful role in shaping their perspective. Help them understand that every situation is an opportunity. They can either see challenges as something happening **to** them or as something happening **for** them. The greatest athletes aren't just those who dominate, they're the ones who develop resilience, work ethic, and a growth mindset because they know that every challenge is a chance to rise. Your support and guidance will help them respond in a healthy and productive way.

If an athlete joins a team expecting special treatment, demanding starting positions, or disregarding the coaching staff, they're doing themselves a disservice. They miss out on the opportunity to grow, develop, and be part of something bigger than themselves. Our role as parents is not just to advocate for our child but to guide them to exhibit humility, teamwork, and to understand that growth happens through challenges, not through comfort.

I believe it's time to move away from the entitlement mindset and welcome the process of learning, growing, and contributing to a team, no matter how good an athlete is. If you want your child to reach their full potential, help them understand that the greatest success comes from the ability to learn from every experience, no matter how big or small.

Conclusion: A Lifelong Passion for the Game

As we've explored in this chapter, moving from the pure joy of playing sports to the dedication and hard work required to succeed at higher levels is a natural progression that many athletes experience. Legendary coaches like John Wooden, Tony Dungy, Pat Summitt, and countless others have demonstrated that success is not just about wins and losses but about nurturing a love for the game as well as athletes' mental well-being. These coaches created environments where players felt valued, supported, and motivated to enjoy the game while still striving for excellence.

So, the lesson is: helping a young athlete develop a genuine love for their sport from an early age will go a long way to establishing the foundation for both long-term success and personal growth. Through this love, athletes can withstand the inevitable challenges that come with higher levels of competition. The process of increasing commitment, developing skills, and understanding the importance of teamwork are all part of the package, and this process must be accompanied by a continued passion for the game.

By balancing the joy of playing with the discipline of improvement, we set up our children for a lifelong engagement with sports, one that is driven by both passion and a growth mindset. Positive reinforcement, a focus on effort over outcomes, and an understanding that the adventure is as important as the end results will ensure that young athletes thrive in ways that extend far beyond the field or court.

Ultimately, victory is not measured only by championships or accolades, but by the love of the game that athletes carry with them throughout their lives. When they stop loving the game, any victory feels hollow.

6

Supporting Your Child Through Success and Failure

Learning to Win: Sophia's Story of Loss and Resilience

Sophia had always been the best player on her high school volleyball team. Since making varsity as a freshman, she had been the go-to outside hitter, the one her teammates trusted in the biggest moments. Now a junior, she was among the top players in the region, with college scouts beginning to take notice. Winning had become an expectation.

But all that changed in the regional championship.

The gym was packed, the air thick with anticipation. Sophia's team, the Westwood Titans, faced their toughest rival, the Ridgeview Storm.

Both teams had battled through a grueling tournament, each match more intense than the last. This was the final hurdle, the match that would decide who advanced to state.

Sophia had been off her game from the start. Her timing was off, her serves lacked precision, and every hit seemed to land just outside the lines. Ridgeview had studied her well, anticipating her every move. The harder she tried to correct herself, the worse she played. By the time the final set arrived, she was unraveling.

Match point. Ridgeview led 14-13. The ball was set perfectly to Sophia, her moment to redeem herself, to do what she had done a hundred times before. She hit it with everything she had.

And missed.

The ball clipped the net and dropped onto her side of the court. Ridgeview erupted in celebration, their cheers drowning out the stunned silence of the Titans' bench. Sophia stood frozen, staring at the ball as if willing time to reverse itself.

Tears burned behind her eyes, but she refused to let them fall. She felt the weight of her teammates' disappointment, the unspoken question hanging in the air: How could she, their leader, have failed them?

That night, Sophia lay in bed, replaying every mistake, every misstep. Doubt crept in. *What if I'm not as good as I thought? What if I never play the same again?*

The next morning, she showed up at the gym early, expecting to be alone. But her coach was already there, sitting on the bleachers, watching as she walked in.

"Didn't think you'd be back so soon," Coach said, her voice calm.

"I have to fix it," Sophia muttered.

Coach nodded. "Good. But first, tell me what went wrong."

Sophia hesitated, then sighed. "I got in my own head. Every mistake made me tighten up more. I wanted to win so badly; I was scared to lose."

Coach gave a knowing smile. "That's the thing, Soph. The best players don't play to avoid losing. They play to win. Big difference."

Sophia thought about that as Coach continued.

"You know what separates great players from good ones? It's not talent, and it's not winning. It's what they do after they fail. If you let this match define you, you'll never recover. But if you let it teach you, you'll come back stronger."

That night at home, her father sat down next to her at the kitchen table, placing a steaming mug of tea in front of her. "You know," he said, his voice steady, "every great athlete has a moment like this, a time when they fall so hard, they wonder if they can get back up."

Sophia stared into her cup. "But what if I can't?"

He smiled. "Then you don't deserve to win yet."

She looked up, confused.

"Winning is easy, Sophia. Losing is where you find out who you really are. If you walk away now, you'll never know what could have happened if you kept going."

Over the next few weeks, Sophia trained harder than ever. She watched film, analyzed her mistakes, and focused on the mental side of the game. Instead of fearing failure, she embraced it while learning that each error was a lesson, each loss an opportunity. Slowly, she felt herself getting better, not just physically, but mentally.

By the time the next season arrived, she was a different player. Not just physically stronger, but mentally tougher.

Failure is inevitable

In sports, failure is inevitable. No athlete, no matter how skilled, disciplined, or determined, escapes defeat. Yet, it is in these moments of struggle that the most valuable lessons are learned. Youth sports serve as a proving ground, not just for athletic ability but for the development of resilience, mental fortitude, and emotional maturity. In my opinion, how an athlete responds to failure often determines their long-term success, both on and off the field.

Thankfully, young athletes rarely have to cope with these moments alone. In the midst of failure, emotions run high, and frustration, self-doubt, and disappointment can cloud judgment, making it difficult to see beyond the immediate setback. This is when a mentor - a coach, a parent, or another trusted figure, becomes invaluable. A mentor provides perspective, reminding the athlete that failure is not the end but a necessary part of growth. They highlight the positives that an athlete might overlook, pointing out the hard work, progress, and effort that hold immense value, even though they did not lead to victory.

A mentor also brings **calm to the storm**, helping young athletes understand that one game, one mistake, or one moment does not define their entire playing career. By reinforcing the idea that setbacks are steppingstones rather than roadblocks, they teach athletes to analyze what went wrong without being consumed by it. Instead of considering failure a negative, young athletes begin to recognize it as an opportunity to improve.

Most importantly, a mentor instills the confidence a young person needs to keep moving forward. Whether it's a coach breaking down film to show how an athlete can adjust, a parent reminding their child of past successes, or a former player sharing their own experiences with failure, the presence of a guiding voice ensures that failure does not lead to fear or frustration, but to resilience. The ability to recover from a setback is not something an athlete learns in isolation; it is nurtured through the steady encouragement, wisdom, and belief of those who have walked the path before them.

A December 2024 article in *The Guardian,* titled "Is it important for kids to learn about winning and losing?" highlights the significance of learning to handle both winning and losing from an early age. In the article, experts stress that while competition can build confidence, it must be balanced with psychological safety to ensure that young athletes develop resilience, humility, and a healthy perspective on success. When children are taught to celebrate their victories with grace and learn from their setbacks without discouragement, they gain skills that extend far beyond the field of play.

As we all know, in youth sports, there are moments of triumph and defeat, and both offer invaluable opportunities for growth. As parents, our role is to help our children manage these experiences in a healthy, constructive way that builds not only their athletic skills but also their emotional resilience and personal character.

In this chapter, we'll discuss how parents can support their children through both the highs and lows of sports, celebrating wins while maintaining humility, helping them handle losses in a way that builds resilience and growth, and equipping them with the mental toughness needed to overcome adversity. By providing the right kind of support, we can ensure that our children learn important life lessons from every experience, both positive and negative.

Celebrating Wins: Building Confidence Without Arrogance

Let's be honest, winning is exciting, no matter the level of competition or the age of the athlete. It's natural for both parents and players to feel a sense of pride with every win; after all, winning is often the tangible result of countless hours of hard work and sacrifice from both parents and athletes. But there is a way to celebrate victories that builds confidence without encouraging arrogance or an elitist attitude. Confidence is important, of course, but humility should always come first.

From my perspective, and based on my years of experience, one of the greatest dangers in sports is when success leads to entitlement.

Young athletes who experience consistent victories, especially those who are naturally gifted or play on dominant teams, can begin to believe that winning is their right rather than a reward earned through effort. This mindset can breed complacency, weaken work ethic, and create an attitude of superiority that alienates teammates, coaches, and even opponents. Worse, when failure inevitably comes, as it does for every athlete, those who have tied their identity solely to winning often struggle to cope, sometimes walking away from the sport entirely, like a sore loser, rather than facing the adversity.

This is why humility is as important as confidence. True confidence isn't about proving superiority over others, it's about trusting in one's ability while respecting the game and those who compete in it. Athletes who approach success with humility recognize that no victory is won alone. They acknowledge their teammates, respect their opponents, and understand that every achievement is built on lessons learned from both wins and losses.

As a coach, I make it a priority to help players celebrate success the right way. I remind them that the moment we start believing we are above the game is the moment we stop growing. I challenge my players to never let success make them comfortable and to never let failure lead them to quit. I encourage them to appreciate victory but also to recognize that the struggles, the lessons, and the character built along the way are all more important than the outcome itself.

Of course, it goes without saying that parents also play a critical role in shaping how their children handle success. When parents focus solely on results, praising only wins and rankings, children internalize the idea that their worth is tied to their ability to win. But when parents emphasize effort, improvement, and sportsmanship, young athletes develop a more balanced perspective. They learn that winning is meaningful, but so is perseverance, teamwork, and respect for others.

In the end, the most successful athletes are not those who accumulate the most trophies, but those who develop the mindset and character to handle both triumph and failure with grace. Yes, winning is rewarding, but how we handle success speaks volumes about who we are as human beings. The best athletes, and the best people, are the ones who can stand on top with humility and reach down to help others rise with them.

As Dr. Carol Dweck explains in *Mindset: The New Psychology of Success*, "When children are praised for their effort, they are more likely to adopt a growth mindset, which encourages them to view challenges as opportunities for growth rather than obstacles." This mindset allows children to pursue success with confidence, rather than the arrogance that comes from focusing only on winning.

In fact, excessive praise or overemphasis on winning can lead to unrealistic expectations and increased pressure, potentially making the child anxious about maintaining their success. We parents need to celebrate the hard work and determination that led to each winning moment. By reinforcing the value of effort, perseverance, and teamwork, we can ensure that our child's confidence is grounded in their process, not just the outcome.

Handling Losses: Teaching Resilience and Growth

There's been a long-standing joke in my family since I was a kid: if I lost - *at anything* - you'd better clear the area because I would be on the warpath. I wasn't just a sore loser; I was a *scorched earth* kind of competitor. Board games? Flipped. Ping pong paddles? Launched at friends. Consolation from my parents? Ignored and dismissed. As I got older, I even started wanting to physically fight people when I lost to them. I was filled with pure, unfiltered, competitive rage. And, unfortunately for my parents, I didn't just take losses hard, I *saw red.*

If I lost, if my team lost, if anything remotely close to losing happened, it was the end of the world in my mind. So, if you're raising a young athlete wired like this, all I can say is… I'm sorry. Buckle up, brace yourself, and maybe reinforce the furniture. But also know this: you're not alone, and there is support. Whether it's talking with a sports psychologist, connecting with a parenting coach, or simply finding community help through your child's team, there are resources to help you handle the emotional roller coaster of raising a passionate competitor. Learning how to reframe tough moments, or watching how other experienced parents provide mentorship, can be a game changer. Remember, supporting your child doesn't mean you have to have all the answers.

Parents play a pivotal role in shaping a "**Find a Way**" mentality in their children. This doesn't mean cushioning them from failure or making excuses when things don't go their way, it means teaching them how to respond. The best thing a parent can do is shift the focus from what happened to what's next.

In my experience, the most successful athletes, and for that matter, the most successful people in life, share one defining trait: they refuse to accept defeat as the final word. No matter the odds, no matter the setbacks, they figure out how to get the job done. It's not always graceful, it's rarely easy, and it's never guaranteed, but they don't stop until they've found a way to succeed.

Trust me, your child is watching how *you* handle adversity. If you blame, complain, or make excuses, they'll mirror your behavior. But if you model adaptability and problem-solving, they'll learn to approach challenges with that same mindset. Winning starts with the belief that there's *always* a way forward.

Reframing Loss as a Learning Opportunity

Losses can feel deeply personal, particularly for competitive athletes who pour their hearts into their sport. A tough defeat can cause frustration, self-doubt, and even feelings of failure. Without the right guidance, these emotions can shake an athlete's confidence, making them question their abilities, love for the game, or even their future in sports. This is why coaches, parents, and mentors play a vital role in shaping how young athletes process and respond to losses.

One of the most important lessons in every athlete's life is understanding the principle of **"controlling the controllables."** I remember teaching this concept to my kids as they grew up playing competitive soccer. Once they truly understood what it meant, it was like a weight had been lifted off their shoulders. They played with more confidence, their focus sharpened, and the stress of performance began to fade. It freed them to be better players, because instead of worrying about things beyond their control, they poured their energy into what they could control.

The reality of competition is that some things will always be out of a player's hands. Bad calls, poor weather conditions, how the opponent plays, or even unexpected issues within their own team; these are all out of a player's control. But the most successful athletes don't waste energy on what they cannot change; they focus entirely on what they can control, which is their own effort, preparation, and mindset.

What Athletes Can Control:

These are the factors that every athlete has direct influence over, regardless of the situation:

Controllable	Description
Effort and Work Ethic	The Intensity and focus put into training, practices, and games
Preparation	Studying scouting reports, watching film, and understanding game strategy
Attitude and Mental Approach	Staying positive, coachable, and locked in during competition
Showing Up on Time	Being punctual and ready to contribute
Discipline and Accountability	Staying committed to personal and team goals
Game-Day Readiness	Quality sleep habits, eating proper foods, and mentally preparing before competition

What Athletes Cannot Control (External Factors):

Uncontrollable	Description
Officiating	Umpires, referees, and judges will make calls, both good and bad.
Weather Conditions	Rain, wind, extreme heat or cold
Opponent's Talent or Preparation	The other team's skills, game plan, or coaching
Crowd or External Noise	Fans, parents, or media opinions
Injuries or Unexpected Setbacks	Injuries are obviously out of an athlete's control

Mastering the "Control the Controllables" Mindset

When athletes learn to let go of distractions and focus only on what they can control, their performance improves, their confidence grows, and they become mentally tougher. Instead of wasting time on excuses or frustrations, they channel their energy into preparation, execution, and resilience.

The best athletes, and the best teams, aren't rattled by what's out of their hands. They put in the work, trust the process, and find a way to win, no matter the circumstances.

Parents who want to help their athlete should take some time to discuss the concept of loss as feedback. Here are some ways you can help your athlete reframe losing and use the information as an opportunity to succeed:

- **Shift the Perspective** – Instead of asking, "Why did I lose?," ask, "What can I learn from this?" Losses expose weaknesses, and that's a good thing - it's a chance to improve.

- **Analyze, Don't Dwell** – Reviewing mistakes isn't about beating yourself up; it's about figuring out what went wrong and how to fix it. Watch film, reflect on key moments, and adjust.

- **Focus on Controllable Factors** – Effort, attitude, preparation, and decision-making are within an athlete's control. Bad calls, weather, or lucky breaks aren't, so don't waste energy on them.

- **Adopt a Growth Mindset** – Instead of thinking, *I'm just not good enough*, tell yourself, *I'm not good enough… yet*. Improvement comes from persistence, not immediate success.

- **Use Frustration as Fuel** – Let the sting of a loss drive you to work harder, not break you down. The best athletes turn frustration into motivation.

- **Recognize That Everyone Loses** – Even the greatest champions have faced tough losses. Michael Jordan was cut from his high school team! Tom Brady lost three Super Bowls. Setbacks are part of life as a winning athlete.

- **Find the Silver Lining** – Maybe the loss exposed a technical flaw you need to fix. Maybe it revealed a weakness in conditioning. Every loss has a lesson, so find it and apply it.

- **Move On with Purpose** – Process the loss, take what you need from it, and move forward. Carrying a loss like baggage into the next game only makes it harder to win.

Building Mental Toughness

Through Loss: Mental toughness is not developed in easy wins; it is forged in moments of adversity. Losses present opportunities for athletes to learn how to handle pressure, overcome setbacks, and push forward despite challenges. Teaching athletes to maintain composure, stay positive, and remain committed to their goals, even after failure, prepares them not just for sports, but for life.

The ability to handle loss with grace and resilience is what separates good athletes from great ones. Those who can embrace adversity, extract lessons from failure, and return with renewed focus will ultimately achieve more than those who crumble under the weight of disappointment.

According to *Sports Psychology Today*, "Parents who foster an environment where children can learn from failure tend to raise more resilient athletes." When children are supported through losses, rather than criticized or belittled, they learn how to bounce back from setbacks. Failure teaches athletes to assess what went wrong, make adjustments, and come back stronger.

For example, after a tough loss, instead of offering immediate advice or trying to fix the situation, let your child express their feelings. Acknowledge their disappointment but also encourage them to look ahead. This way, they develop emotional intelligence to handle future challenges.

Tools for Overcoming Adversity: While we're talking about mental toughness, let's drill down a little to more fully define what it means. Mental toughness is the ability to stay calm under pressure, to keep going when things get tough, and to persevere despite obstacles. Building this trait is vital for athletes, and it's something that can be nurtured through supportive parenting.

Dr. Michael Gervais, a sports psychologist who works with elite athletes, describes mental toughness as the ability to "remain focused and determined, regardless of the circumstances." This quality is critical for athletes who face adversity, whether it's a losing streak, an injury, or a difficult competition. Mental toughness helps athletes recover from setbacks and continue working toward their goals, no matter the challenges.

There are several ways we parents can support the development of mental toughness in our children:

- **Encourage Positive Self-Talk:** Teach your child to use affirming, positive language when faced with adversity. Instead of focusing on mistakes or failures, encourage them to say, "I'll learn from this" or "I'm getting better with each practice" or "I'm getting better at this skill."

- **Develop Coping Strategies:** Help your child develop coping strategies for managing stress and frustration. This could involve breathing exercises, visualization techniques, or even journaling about their experiences. These tools often help athletes stay calm and focused during competition and training.

- **Foster a Growth Mindset**: As we've learned, a growth mindset is the foundation of mental toughness. Reinforce the idea that skills can be developed through effort, and challenges are an opportunity for improvement. This mindset will encourage your child to stay positive even when the going gets tough.

Avoid Burnout

"Burnout," according to *Merriam-Webster Dictionary*, is "Exhaustion of physical or emotional strength or motivation, usually as a result of prolonged stress or frustration."

In today's competitive sports culture, the expectation to win or recover quickly from losses can be overwhelming, especially for young athletes. The pressure to constantly perform at a high level, often fueled by external expectations from parents, coaches, and even peers, can take a toll on a child's mental and physical health. One of the leading causes of burnout in young athletes is the chronic stress induced by unrealistic expectations, which can lead to physical exhaustion, mental fatigue, and a diminished passion for the sport. The all-too-common "win-at-all-costs" mentality, coupled with the desire to quickly rebound after a setback, increases the likelihood that athletes will experience burnout.

Burnout in youth sports doesn't always manifest as an obvious collapse but can often present itself as apathy, loss of motivation, or disinterest in the sport. If young people feel they are not allowed to fail or experience moments of imperfection, they may develop a negative relationship with the sport and even choose to quit altogether. This can be compounded by long-term mental health issues, like anxiety and depression, which can stem from feeling constantly under pressure to perform.

Signs of Burnout in Young Athletes:

- Loss of enthusiasm or enjoyment for the sport they once loved

- Increased anxiety or irritability before practices or games

- Complaints of chronic fatigue, soreness, or frequent injuries

- Drop in performance despite continued effort

- A desire to quit or avoid conversations about the sport

Burnout happens when the joy of the game is replaced by stress and obligation. Some young athletes fear disappointing their parents, coaches, or teammates, leading them to push through exhaustion instead of recognizing when they need rest.

How Parents and Coaches Can Prevent Burnout:

- Encourage Rest and Recovery: Ensure kids have breaks, both during the season and in the offseason. Overtraining leads to physical exhaustion and mental fatigue.

- Allow for Multi-Sport or Free Play: Specializing too early in one sport can contribute to burnout and overuse injuries. Encourage your kids to try different activities to keep sports fresh and fun.

- Check in on Their Motivation: Instead of assuming they want to keep playing at a high level, ask them, "Are you still enjoying this?" or "What's your favorite part of playing?" If their answers reveal stress or reluctance, it may be time to adjust expectations.

- Keep the Bigger Picture in Mind: Remind them that their identity is not tied to their performance. Reinforce the idea that their sport is merely something they do, not who they are.

Practical Strategies for Post-Game Conversations

One of the most crucial moments for a young athlete's development occurs right after the game: the car ride home. This is when kids are most vulnerable to external pressure, whether they won or lost. How parents handle this moment can make a lasting impact.

What to Say After a Game:

- "I love watching you play." – This simple phrase removes pressure and affirms to them that your support isn't tied to their performance.

- "How do you feel about the game?" – Let them lead the conversation instead of immediately giving feedback.

- "What was the most fun part today?" – Help them focus on enjoyment, not just results.

- "Is there anything you learned from this game?" – Encourage growth without focusing on mistakes.

- "Do you want to talk about the game, or just relax for now?" – Give them control over the conversation.

What to Avoid Saying After a Game:

- "Why did you make that mistake?" – They're already aware of their own errors; pointing them out only increases pressure and upsets them.

- "You should have tried harder." – They may very well have been trying their hardest. Help them focus on growth instead of criticizing their effort.

- "The referee/coach/teammates were unfair." – Blaming external factors teaches kids to make excuses rather than take responsibility.

- "We need to work on that as soon as we get home." – Work to keep the game separate from the rest of their life. They need time to mentally reset and engage in other activities.

Conclusion: Growing Through Success and Failure

The life of an athlete is filled with both triumphs and setbacks, each offering valuable lessons. As parents, coaches, and mentors, our role is not to shield these people from failure, but to guide them through it, helping them recognize that setbacks are opportunities. Teaching resilience, mental toughness, and the value of self-reflection will equip young athletes not only to overcome obstacles but to emerge stronger with each obstacle they face.

In sport and in life, it's not the victories that shape us most, but the lessons learned through adversity. By supporting our children, we can help them build the emotional and mental fortitude they need to succeed, both on and off the field. The true measure of success is not in avoiding failure, but in having the courage to rise after each fall and continue moving forward with determination.

7

The Coach's Role

Once, after a preseason game when I was coaching a high school varsity team, a parent approached me, furious, threatening to withdraw his support for the rest of the year.

The night before, I had sent a message to both the varsity and JV parent groups, asking for volunteers to arrive early and help set up the outfield fence and prepare the stadium. This parent showed up, greeted me warmly, and seemed genuinely happy to help. But after the game, his demeanor had completely changed. His child hadn't played, and I realized that his willingness to lend a hand had come with unspoken expectations.

Over the years, I've thought a lot about that moment, not just about his anger, but about the impossible position he had put his child in. His child was a person of strong character, hardworking, humble, and well-respected, but they were not a first-string player.

More than a decade later, I ran into that same parent at a local pizza shop. It was awkward. The tension in the air felt just as thick as the day he had confronted me. We stood in the small lobby for what felt like an eternity before he finally turned to me and let it all out. He told me how much my decision had hurt him, how he had never let it go.

I didn't argue. I didn't justify or explain. I just listened.

When he finished, I simply said, "I did what I thought was best at the time. I never had malicious intentions."

Silence.

Then, as his pizza order was called, he looked at me, gave a small nod, and muttered something that sounded like an apology. To be honest, I don't remember his exact words, but I know it was something along those lines. And he walked out.

That moment stuck with me. It reminded me that we coaches are human, too. We make decisions based on what's best for the team, not out of favoritism, punishment, or malice. But the weight of those decisions follows us. We carry them long after the games are over, long after the parents and players have moved on. What some see as just another lineup decision or playing-time call can turn into years of resentment. But at the end of the day, all we can do is coach with integrity and make decisions we believe are in the best interest of the players' development on and off the field.

The Power of Trusting the Process

A great example of stepping back and allowing a young athlete to trust the process is the story of Richard Williams and his daughters, legendary tennis champions Venus and Serena Williams. Richard made the intentional decision to pull them back from intensive junior competition at an early age to focus on their personal growth and long-term development. As detailed in the book *King Richard's Story* and numerous interviews, he emphasized patience and longevity while deliberately opting out of early rankings and circuit play.

The Williams sisters rise to greatness didn't come through early professionalization or relentless competition. Instead, it came through calculated patience, grounded in love, balance, and resilience. By trusting the process, Richard allowed his daughters to develop their technical skills, build mental toughness, and cultivate a deep love for the game without the pressure and burnout that often plague young athletes.

Venus and Serena's story is a powerful reminder that patience and perspective can be just as important as talent. It shows what's possible when parents prioritize long-term growth over immediate results.

Trusting the Coach Means Trusting the Journey

When you put your child's development into the hands of a coach, you are making a significant decision to trust that coach. You're not just handing your child over for practices and games, you're entrusting that coach with your child's physical, mental, and emotional development.

A good coach isn't just teaching skills and strategies; they are shaping character, instilling discipline, and helping young athletes cope with challenges both on and off the field. The lessons learned through sports, e.g. handling adversity, working within a team, and striving for improvement, can last a lifetime.

At the end of the day, the best thing a parent can do is allow their child to be coached. The experience may not always look the way you thought it would, but sometimes, the struggles and challenges encountered are the things that help prepare our children for their greatest success.

But trust is a two-way street. Just as coaches commit to developing each athlete in their care, parents must also recognize that growth doesn't always come in the form of immediate success or the playing time they and their children might hope for. Sometimes, the most valuable lessons come from struggle, perseverance, and learning to embrace a role within the team, even when it's not a first-string position. All young athletes benefit when their parents allow coaches to challenge and develop them.

Of course, as much as parents place trust in coaches, that trust can be tested when things don't go as hoped, whether it's a loss, a tough coaching decision, or their child's role on the team. This is where a parent's approach matters most. To me, one of the most beneficial things you can do as a parent is support your child's coach, no matter what age, level of play, or stage of life they are in.

The relationship between parents and coaches plays a pivotal role in the development of young athletes, shaping their character both on and off the field. Coaches not only provide mentorship, teach sportsmanship, and hone athletic skills, but often have a lasting positive influence on an athlete's life (just as my high school baseball coach, Brent Child, did for me). When parents support this role, it strengthens the child's individual growth, teaching valuable lessons about leadership, respect, and how to respond to decisions made by those in positions of authority. Children need to understand that relationships, and how we handle them, are far more important than complaints about playing time, practice schedules, team roster changes, and other temporary frustrations. When parents and coaches work together effectively, they create an environment that nurtures the athletes and sets them up for success in life.

As a coach, I always find it interesting to watch each parent's true character reveal itself over the course of a season. At the start, most parents present themselves as supportive, engaged, and committed to their child's success. But as the season unfolds, through wins and losses, playing-time decisions, and moments of adversity, their true mindset and priorities become evident.

Some parents remain unwaveringly supportive, trusting the process and recognizing that the season is about growth, development, and teamwork, not just individual success. Others, however, begin to exhibit a more self-serving agenda, viewing the team through the lens of their child's role rather than the collective good.

The way a parent handles difficult situations, whether it's a tough loss, a reduced role for their child, or a disagreement with coaching decisions, often speaks volumes. Some will use it as an opportunity to teach their child resilience and accountability, but others will react with frustration, blame, or even engage in subtle attempts to sow dissension among other parents.

I know this firsthand, not just as a coach, but as a parent. I watched my own daughter struggle on a team, not getting the playing time I thought she deserved. Later, she was cut from her high school team, a devastating moment for any athlete and their family. As a father, I felt the sting of her disappointment. At the time, I was frustrated. I knew how hard she had worked, and it was difficult to understand why she wasn't being given the opportunity I thought she'd earned. But I had to check myself and ask if I was reacting as a coach, or as a parent who simply wanted the best for his child.

I had a choice: I could complain, blame the coach, or dwell on what I felt was unfair, or I could support her, help her see the bigger picture, and use this as a lesson in resilience. I chose the latter. We talked about handling adversity, about how setbacks don't define you, how they can, in fact, shape you into something stronger. She learned to face challenges head-on, to work harder, to focus on what she could control rather than what she couldn't. And because of that, she grew, not just as an athlete, but as a person.

That experience reinforced for me that my role as a parent in sports isn't just about ensuring my child gets what they want in the moment. It's about preparing them for all the challenges they will face in life, both on and off the field.

Ultimately, a season doesn't just test the players, it tests the parents as well. It shows who truly believes in the value of sports as a tool for growth and who is more concerned with personal gain. As a coach, I've discovered that managing these dynamics is just as important as coaching the game itself.

In my experience, over the course of a full season, you can usually break a parent group into thirds.

The top third are the parents of players who start and play most of the time. For obvious reasons, these parents are generally the most content and satisfied. They tend to cheer on the team, offer support when asked, and maintain a positive relationship with the coaching staff. Since their child is playing regularly, there's less tension, and they often trust the process without much pushback.

The middle third includes parents whose children are competing for playing time. Their child might start some games and come off the bench in others. These parents usually begin the season supportive, hopeful, and engaged. However, as the season progresses, a few may begin to exhibit frustration, especially if they feel their child isn't getting a fair shot. This is the group where you can find a couple of "sleepers," which are parents who appear supportive early on, but by the end of the season tend to become vocal or dissatisfied if things don't go the way they had hoped in the beginning.

The bottom third are the parents of players who see limited playing time. Within this group, you might find one or two parents who understand the bigger picture. They remain supportive of their child and the team, even though their child isn't on the field much. They understand the value of the team experience, hard work, and character development. Unfortunately, though, most of the parents in this group are the ones who present the greatest challenge to a coach. They tend to question coaching decisions, complain (sometimes publicly), and often act in ways that are divisive and counterproductive to team unity. They usually require extra time and attention. As a result, they make an already demanding job even more difficult for the whole coaching staff.

Beyond these three segments, I've also observed distinct parenting styles that tend to emerge over the course of a season and across all levels of youth and high school sports. Understanding these patterns isn't about labeling others, but about gaining awareness. Hopefully, this will help you reflect on your own approach, recognize what's healthy and what's unhelpful, and ensure you and your child have a fulfilling season.

- **The Helper** (Team-Focused) – These parents are the lifeblood of team culture and operations. They're the first to raise their hand when volunteers are needed. Whether it's organizing snacks, coordinating carpools, helping with fundraisers, or managing team communications, their support is consistent, humble, and never driven by a personal agenda. They show up early, stay late, and step in without needing recognition.

  The Helper is **often the parent that coaches quietly count on** when things become chaotic, they help smooth out logistics so the coach can focus on coaching, and the players can focus on playing. Helpers build bridges between parents and staff, creating a sense of community that benefits everyone. Their presence sends a meaningful message to their child: "We're in this together."

  *Note regarding "The Helper Parent":

- According to research by Wiersma and Fifer, the most impactful parents in youth sports provide low-pressure support when they show up, help where needed, and let the coaches coach. Studies also show that when parents take on constructive, communal roles such as volunteering or assisting with team needs, it strengthens team unity and helps young athletes feel more connected to the experience. Research from the National Academy of Athletics affirms that this kind of healthy, engaged support enhances team cohesion and fosters a greater sense of belonging for everyone. These are the parents who leave a lasting, positive imprint, not just on their own child, but on the entire team environment.

- **The Anchor** (Supporter) – These parents stand by the team and coaching decisions, regardless of the situation or circumstances. They trust the process and focus on their child's growth, not just outcomes.

- **The Scout (The Insider Expert)** – These parents pride themselves on knowing the landscape and who the top players are in the league, which teams are strong, what tendencies opposing coaches lean on, and what strategies might work best. They're always scouting the competition, analyzing matchups, and offering tactical suggestions, often in the form of "helpful tips" to the coaching staff. Sometimes, their insight can be valuable, especially if they have a background in the sport or close connections to local teams. But more often, their unsolicited input becomes overwhelming and unwelcome. Coaches may feel second-guessed or even undermined, especially when the Scout consistently inserts opinions on strategy, playing time, or in-game decisions. What starts as enthusiasm can quickly feel like interference. The key for Scout parents is to pause and ask themselves: *Does the coach want or need this information?* If not, it's best to step back and let the coaching staff lead. When they do share, it should be in the right setting, with the right tone, and only if it's clearly welcomed.

- **The Over-Analyzer (The Stat Rat)** – These parents track everything. Before tryouts are even over, they've already emailed a spreadsheet of their child's stats to include hits, goals, blocks, miles run, personal bests, and often several other categories that have little bearing on team selection or strategy. Once the season starts, they shift into overdrive and analyze every play, every possession, and every box score like a data analyst preparing for a board meeting. No stat is too obscure, and no moment of the game escapes their attention. While some stat-minded parents offer useful insights now and then, especially when invited into an official stat-keeping or analytics role, most coaches are quickly overwhelmed when these numbers are offered unsolicited. The truth is, there's a place for good data. When a coach asks for help tracking trends or measuring success, a parent with analytical skills can be a tremendous asset, but only when invited.

- **The Snowplow** (Over-Involved) – These parents will not allow their child to face adversity or solve problems on their own. They are the ones who carry their child's bags and rush to the sideline with a bottle of water and food during games. They are overly involved and intervene too early for their child; they avoid failure at all costs and will be the one making all the decisions, not their child. Being in total control is important to them.

- **The VIP** (Entitled) – These parents are convinced their child deserves special treatment and exceptions. Although they believe in rules, the rules do not apply to them or their child.

- **The Ghost** (Absent Parent) – These parents are largely uninvolved. They rarely attend games, don't show up to parent meetings, and have little to no communication with the coaching staff. Their child is expected to manage everything alone—logistics, emotions, and challenges—without much support or guidance. On the surface, they may seem "hands-off" in a good way, but their absence creates a void that can leave their child feeling unsupported and disconnected from the team environment.

- **The Snake** (Manipulator) – These are the most time-consuming and challenging parents to deal with. They present themselves as supportive but operate with a "what's in it for me" mindset. When things don't go their way, they spread negativity among other parents, attempting to undermine what the coach has worked hard to build.

- **The Virus** (Disruptor) – These parents become increasingly difficult if their child isn't the star or doesn't receive the playing time they believe is deserved. Their frustration builds throughout the season, sometimes to the point where they become openly divisive, or even leave before the season ends.

- **The Investor** (Transactional Supporter) – These parents often volunteer their time, donate money, or help cover big-ticket items like team trips or gear. On the surface, their support seems generous, and in many ways, it is. But underneath, there's often an unspoken expectation: that their child will receive more playing time, a leadership role, or special consideration in return. If that doesn't happen, anger sets in. What began as generosity can quickly become transactional, leading to tension between the parent and coaching staff, and sometimes resentment among other parents.

Every season of most sports includes a blend of these dynamics. So, where do you fit in? Which of these seven parent types best reflects your approach, or where you find yourself right now?

As we move on in this chapter, we will talk about how parents can build positive relationships with coaches, understand the different coaching styles that may influence their children, and learn when to step in or stay out of the way. Additionally, we will discuss the dangers of "helicopter parenting" and the negative impact that overly involved parents can have on their child's athletic development and well-being.

Building Positive Relationships with Coaches

Most of us know that a positive relationship is characterized by mutual trust, respect, support, and effective communication.

From a coach's perspective, **the ideal parent** is one who respects team rules, ensures their child is prepared with the necessary equipment and apparel, and recognizes the coach as a dedicated mentor who is investing time and energy into developing young athletes. An ideal parent acknowledges the coach's expertise, trusts their ability to teach and lead, and remains supportive of coaching decisions. They also contribute to the team's success by assisting with needs such as fundraising, scorekeeping, or field maintenance, all while understanding and respecting the boundaries between parent and coach.

The foundation of a strong coach-parent relationship is **mutual respect**. Building a positive partnership begins with recognizing that coaches have the athletes' best interests at heart. Their role is to teach skills, strategies, and discipline, and often these extend beyond the sport itself. When parents acknowledge a coach's expertise and reinforce their decisions, they are helping to create a unified front and set an example for their child by modeling consistency in values, expectations, and best interests of the athlete.

Understanding a Coach's Commitment: Time, Pay, and Perspective

Coaching at any level demands far more than just knowledge of the game. It involves long hours of preparation, emotional investment, and administrative duties, often with little financial reward. Whether coaching youth teams, club programs, or high school athletes, most coaches do it because they care deeply about kids and the game, not because they are well compensated.

Even when coaches are paid, the time they invest far outweighs the paycheck. According to a 2025 ZipRecruiter report:

- **Youth and Club Coaches** typically earn an average of **$18.80/hour**, ranging from $10.10 to $36.54. Many work **9 to 30 hours a week** during the season, with earnings that often total just **$3,000–$4,000 for an entire season**.

- **High School Coaches** often put in **60 hours a week during the season**, plus **20–30 hours off-season**, yet earn around **$24.90/hour**. Over a 12-week season, that amounts to **720+ hours** for a seasonal paycheck of roughly **$18,000** and that's without calculating the off-season hours.

Why This Matters

Before questioning a coach's decisions or commitment, I think we all need to remember what they take home and what they give up to be there. Most coaches juggle full-time jobs, family responsibilities, and countless behind-the-scenes duties: practices, games, travel, film review, player development, team culture, parent communication, and more.

So, if we break it down, many coaches earn just a few dollars per hour, if that. It's my hope that understanding this will help shift mindsets from criticism to appreciation, because the truth is that most coaches are not in it for the paycheck; they're in it to mentor and shape young lives.

Respect, Boundaries, and Communication

Because a coach is visible on the sidelines, they can be an easy target for some parents, who take them for granted. But strong parent-coach relationships are built through **respectful, timely communication**, not sideline confrontations or emotionally charged critiques.

Clear boundaries protect both sides. For example, I once had a parent confront me right after a tough loss, upset about their child's playing time. Had they followed our team's 48-hour policy and encouraged their child to advocate for themselves first, they would've discovered that their child had asked to sit out the game because of an injury. Instead of an emotional confrontation, a calm, respectful conversation would've enlightened the parent about the reality. This experience reinforced why respecting team procedures and choosing the right moment to address concerns is fundamental to maintaining a healthy parent-coach relationship.

Clear, constructive communication that keeps in mind the coach's workload makes the parent-coach partnership far more effective and positive for everyone, especially the athlete.

For example, not every issue requires an immediate response. Late-night text messages, calls during a coach's personal time, or unexpected sideline confrontations disrupt the coach's ability to focus. Concerns should be addressed at the appropriate time and in a manner that promotes constructive dialogue rather than unnecessary tension.

Most programs have established procedures for handling concerns. In many cases, players are encouraged to speak with the coach about any issues before their parents become involved. If the concern remains unresolved or parents feel further discussion is necessary, then by all means, they should feel free to schedule a meeting with the coach at an appropriate time. Respecting this process ensures communication remains professional and productive.

Of course, if a parent suspects any form of abuse, misconduct, or a situation that puts their child and/or others in danger, obviously they should act immediately. In such cases, it's perfectly acceptable to bypass the standard communication process and report the concern directly to the coach or the appropriate authority, such as the league president, head of coaching, or athletic director. But parents need to use their best judgment to distinguish between common team concerns and serious issues that require urgent attention.

Ultimately, the best parent-coach relationships are built on trust, patience, and an understanding of the bigger picture. Coaches commit themselves to developing young athletes because they love what they do, but they cannot do it alone. Parents who respect the coaching role, support their efforts, and maintain healthy boundaries contribute not only to their child's success but also to the overall health of the team. By working together, coaches and parents can create a positive and productive athletic experience for everyone involved.

For those of you wondering how to forge a healthy relationship with your child's coach, building positive communication begins at home, in private conversations with your child.

One year a player approached me before practice, their face filled with worry. They wanted me to know that the hateful remarks about me that had been posted online the night before weren't from their parents. I could see the weight of the situation pressing down on this athlete, who was a great kid, about to graduate high school, and yet here this young person was, feeling the need to clean up a mess.

I didn't say anything, but I knew the truth. This player's parents had, in fact, posted the comments. Their bitter complaints about playing time and my coaching decisions weren't just whispers behind the scenes; days earlier, they had thrown the very same words at me that had been posted online. And now, their child was caught in the crossfire, burdened with stress no child should carry.

I saw how it affected this player, who was afraid that I would hold the actions of their parents against them, and they would somehow pay the price. No athlete should have to cope with this kind of weight.

I'm not saying this is common behavior among parents, but I am asking for all parents to please be mindful of the impact your words and actions have, not just on the coach, but on the person who matters most: your child.

Coaching Styles: How to Work with Different Approaches

In my view, one of the best things a parent can do to help their child is to understand how their coach operates: how they think, respond, and make decisions. The first and most important question parents should ask themselves from the beginning of the season to the end is:

Is what I'm seeing, hearing, and experiencing real, or do I have a skewed perception?

As we all know, perception isn't always reality. Yet it's easy for someone to form an opinion about a coach based on feelings or past negative experiences with other coaches, without taking the time to investigate or consider the evidence before reaching a conclusion. For instance, a parent once approached me, visibly frustrated, because their child, who had typically been a starter on previous teams, had been placed in the position of closer in the pitching rotation. The parents assumed that this decision meant their child wasn't being valued or trusted as much as they had been in the past. They didn't understand why their child was now being put in a role they considered secondary.

But my reasoning had been based on the needs of the team. With a full pitching staff and a lineup of talented new players, the team needed someone with a calm demeanor and the ability to finish strong under pressure, someone who could hold onto a lead and close out games. The closer role wasn't a demotion; in fact, it was one of the most crucial roles on the team. I explained that this would help the player develop important skills, such as handling high-pressure situations and supporting the team in critical moments, all vital aspects of becoming a well-rounded player.

Once I took the time to explain my philosophy on team success and how the closer fit into the bigger picture, the parent understood. They saw how this opportunity could help their child grow and were happy with the decision. The perception that their child was being sidelined quickly turned into appreciation for the chance to develop more skills, and they left with a renewed trust in my strategy for the team.

This example illustrates how easily parents can misinterpret a coaching decision when they're unaware of the broader team needs or the growth opportunities available for their child. By taking the time to communicate the reasoning behind decisions, coaches can help parents see the bigger picture, and this can only benefit them and their child.

Understanding different coaching styles is equally important, since this knowledge will help you provide the right support, regardless of the coach's approach. Each style has both challenges and benefits, and how you respond can significantly influence your child's development.

Let's examine how these coaching styles play out in practice and how parents can best support their child in each setting.

Types of Coaching Styles

The Authoritarian (Command) Coach

This coach is highly disciplined, sets strict rules, and expects athletes to follow instructions without questioning decisions. They prioritize structure, hard work, and winning.

- **How It Affects Your Child:**
  - Provides clear expectations and discipline
  - Can develop mental toughness and accountability
  - May limit creativity and reduce a child's sense of autonomy

- **How to Parent in This Environment:**
  - Reinforce the importance of discipline, structure, and respect for authority.
  - Encourage your child to embrace the approach but be an open listener to ensure they feel heard.
  - If concerns arise, approach the coach with respect and engage in constructive dialogue rather than confrontation.

The Democratic (Cooperative) Coach

This coach values input from players, encourages discussion, and fosters teamwork. They emphasize skill development and personal growth rather than just winning.

- **How It Affects Your Child:**
  - Promotes confidence and independence

- o Teaches decision-making and leadership
- o May lead to inconsistency if athletes aren't accustomed to self-direction

- **How to Parent in This Environment:**
  - o Support your child in taking responsibility for their development.
  - o Avoid micromanaging; let them engage with the coach themselves and learn through experience.
  - o Encourage open communication but reinforce that the coach is the leader.

The Non-Assertive (Submissive) Coach

This coach provides minimal guidance, allowing players to self-direct and learn through trial and error. They are largely hands-off and serve more as a resource than a leader.

- **How It Affects Your Child:**
  - o Encourages self-motivation and responsibility
  - o Can be beneficial for highly driven athletes but confusing for those who need structure
  - o May lead to frustration if athletes feel unsupported

- **How to Parent in This Environment:**
  - o Help your child develop their own motivation and goals.
  - o Encourage self-discipline and leadership.
  - o Step in with guidance when necessary, but don't take over the coaching role.

The Holistic (Person-Centered) Coach

This coach focuses on the whole athlete, mentally, emotionally, and physically. They emphasize long-term personal growth over short-term wins and often incorporate life lessons into their coaching.

- **How It Affects Your Child:**
    - Builds confidence, resilience, and personal growth
    - Encourages well-rounded development beyond just sports
    - May not push for maximum competitiveness, which some parents find frustrating

- **How to Parent in This Environment:**
    - Align with the coach's philosophy by encouraging emotional intelligence and growth.
    - Focus on the bigger picture, character development, leadership, and teamwork.
    - Support the process rather than obsessing over immediate success or playing time.

A Word About Parent Coaches

Experienced, fair, and dedicated parent coaches can be an incredible asset for every player and parent on the team. This type of coach is truly worth their weight in gold. They are deeply invested in the growth and development of every player, not just their own child. Because they have a personal stake in the team's success, they understand that when the players around their child thrive, their own child benefits as well. This perspective often leads to a deep commitment to fairness, team unity, and long-term development for all players.

Naturally, there can be a downside to this dynamic when a parent coach's priorities become too focused on their own child. A selfish parent coach, one who is primarily motivated by creating opportunities or guaranteeing playing time for their own child, can unintentionally harm not only their child's development but also the entire team environment. This can breed resentment among players and parents, damage team morale, and undermine the coach's credibility.

I've witnessed both scenarios firsthand. I've seen parent coaches who embody fairness and dedication, leading their teams with integrity and fostering a positive atmosphere where all players feel valued. I've also seen parent coaches whose self-interest negatively impacts the team, causing division and frustration that linger well beyond the season.

Ultimately, the key difference comes down to mindset and motivation: whether the coach views their role as serving the entire team or simply advancing their own family's interests. For parents, understanding this dynamic can help you better support your child and navigate the challenges that come with having a parent coach on the sidelines.

Understanding the Coach Beyond Their Style

The deeper factors that shape who a coach is and how they lead are equally important considerations. Too often, parents form opinions based solely on surface-level interactions or how much playing time their child receives. But before drawing conclusions about whether a coach is "good" or "bad," it's worth looking at the bigger picture.

A coach's effectiveness isn't defined by one decision or a single season but shaped by a combination of their knowledge of the game, years of experience, leadership style, internal motivations, and how they handle adversity. Some coaches are tacticians, others are motivators or builders of character (some may be a mix of both). Some are new to coaching and still growing themselves. And while you might not always agree with their decisions, don't forget to ask: **What is this coach trying to accomplish, and how are they going about it?**

The danger is in forming a judgment too quickly, based on frustration, hearsay, or assumptions, without understanding the full context. When parents take time to see the coach for who they are as a person, they often gain perspective, even if they don't agree with every decision. And that perspective can go a long way in supporting both their child's experience and the team's overall health.

Warning Signs to Watch for in Coaches

While we never want to judge a coach too quickly, there are also legitimate warning signs that we as parents should be aware of. Here are a few red flags to watch for as you try to understand the heart, motivation, and maturity of the coach who is leading your child:

- **The Inexperienced but Impressive Athlete-Turned-Coach**

  Sometimes, former athletes step into coaching roles right after their playing careers end. On the surface, this can seem like a great opportunity and after all, they know the (current) game and may have impressive résumés. But I probably don't need to tell you that being a great athlete doesn't automatically translate into being a great leader of young people. These coaches may lack the maturity, emotional awareness, or developmental mindset needed to guide children well. They might be very good at the skills they are teaching but lack the ability to break down and teach the mechanics and nuances of the movements and tasks. They might push too hard, struggle to communicate effectively, or fail to see the importance of shaping character in addition to performance. When they don't have the proper foundation, their influence can sometimes do more harm than good.

- **The Over-Coacher**

  Some coaches mistake intensity for excellence and coach far beyond the development level of their team. They run their teams like professional programs as they overload the schedule with daily practices, constant games, and nonstop drills. They teach advanced systems and complex techniques to players who haven't even mastered the basics. And while structure, repetition, and discipline do have their place in development, these coaches often miss the point: kids aren't pros, and youth sports should not look or feel like a military boot camp.

These coaches rarely leave room for creativity, spontaneity, or fun. They demand robotic execution and treat the game like a scripted performance rather than a dynamic, ever-changing experience. It's as if they're holding a video game joystick, controlling every movement, yelling out instructions on where to go, what to do, and how to act and never allowing the athlete to think, feel, or express themselves freely within the game.

- **The Self-Serving Coach**

  This may be the most dangerous kind of coach your child can play for and it happens to be my number one personal (coaching) pet peeve: **the coach who is in it for themselves.**

  These coaches don't view their role as a calling to serve young people; they treat it as a steppingstone to something greater. For them, the team is simply a platform or a stage to chase recognition, rack up wins, or climb the ladder to their next opportunity. Players and parents are merely pawns in their personal pursuit of status.

  These coaches often lack any real connection with the kids in their care. They don't see them as whole people with hearts, dreams, struggles, and potential beyond the game. Instead, players become numbers on a roster, tools to be used for as long as they're useful.

When a player isn't performing to the standard of these coaches, needs extra development, or doesn't fit the mold, they move on from them. These coaches have a *throwaway mindset*. They see every player as disposable and replaceable, operating with the mindset that there's always someone waiting in the wings who might better serve their system. They coach for output, not for impact.

They also tend to keep parents at arm's length by avoiding interaction, withholding communication, and treating the parent-child bond as a distraction rather than a vital support system. They don't see the player as part of a bigger story that includes a family, a set of values, and a life outside the sport.

Here's the irony: many of these coaches think they're acting like elite coaches. They try to mimic what they perceive as a "college-level" or "professional" coaching style. But they get it wrong. Because most of the greatest college and professional coaches in the world don't treat their athletes this way. In fact, the best among them understand that relationships, communication, and trust are essential to high performance. They lead with connection, not control. They motivate through belief, not fear. They develop the person, not just the player.

This type of coach has a major misconception about what great coaching should be. They think intensity equals impact, and control equals leadership. But they're missing the mark and doing real damage to the athletes they're supposed to be serving.

So, if you're a parent, and your child's coach shows no interest in who your child is beyond the field, doesn't ask questions, doesn't build trust, doesn't care, then take note. That's a major red flag.

And if you're a coach reading this, take a hard look at yourself:

- Are you coaching to elevate kids, or elevate yourself?
- Do you invest in the development of the players you have, or constantly look past them for the next one?
- Do you think you're modeling elite coaching, or are you simply imitating what you believe is elite coaching?
- Do you engage with parents as part of the process, or treat them like obstacles?

I have to say this to any coach reading this – *If you're not building the person behind the jersey, you're not coaching.*

Main Takeaways for Parents

- **Be adaptable**. Each coach is different, and your child will benefit from learning under multiple styles.

- **Teach resilience.** Help your child understand that challenges are opportunities for growth.

- **Communicate wisely.** If you have concerns, approach the coach with respect and seek understanding before reacting emotionally.

- **Encourage independence.** Let your child take ownership of their experience and advocate for themselves when needed.

Additionally, take the time to reflect on your own personality, past experiences, and expectations as a parent. If you were an athlete yourself, you may naturally gravitate toward, or clash with, certain coaching styles. If you're a CEO, executive, or high-level professional, you might expect efficiency, accountability, and high performance, which could create tension when you're dealing with a more relaxed coaching approach. If you're a working-class parent, you might value toughness, work ethic, and perseverance, which could make it frustrating if a coach is too lenient or unstructured. An easy-going and laid-back person might clash with an authoritarian coach who expects everyone to be on time, highly disciplined, and fully committed.

As many of us already know, our personal experiences shape how we view our child's life in sports. Recognizing our own tendencies allows us to step back and ensure we're reacting in a way that benefits our child rather than imposing our own expectations on their experience. I believe the best approach is to support our children while allowing them to manage their own relationship with the coach.

Let's face it, the best young athletes aren't just shaped by their talent or their coaches, they are shaped by the support and mindset instilled in them by their parents. When parents and coaches work together with a mutual understanding of roles and expectations, it creates an environment where young athletes can thrive, both in sports and beyond.

When to Step In and When to Stay Out: Boundaries with Coaches

Knowing when to step in and when to step back is part of finding that balance between being a supportive parent and respecting the coach's role. It's natural for parents to want the best for their children, but over-involvement can strain relationships with coaches and, more importantly, hinder a child's ability to develop independence. Of course, there are times when stepping in is not only justified but necessary, which we'll also talk about.

Ultimately, the decision to intervene is deeply personal. **Only you, as a parent, can determine when a situation crosses a line**, when coaching goes from being tough but constructive to being harmful and unconstructive. While every coach has their own style, there are certain behaviors that may be concerning and warrant a conversation, depending on the age and maturity level of your child.

Age and Context Matter

The circumstances that might cause concern are different at different stages of a child's life in athletics.

- **For young athletes (ages 5-12),** coaches are shaping early experiences in sports. If a coach swears or uses other colorful language excessively, makes inappropriate jokes, or uses negative reinforcement, it may be necessary to step in. A child at this stage is still forming their confidence and love for the game, and a toxic environment will almost certainly be detrimental.

- **For middle school athletes (ages 12-14),** coaching styles often become more demanding. But there's a difference between a coach holding players accountable and degrading them. If you think your child is receiving harsh criticism that seems personal or discouraging rather than constructive, you might want to assess whether their growth and enjoyment of sport are being compromised.

- **For high school athletes (ages 15+),** players should be developing the skills to advocate for themselves. A coach yelling out of intensity is different from a coach belittling or embarrassing a player. At this stage, the decision to intervene should be carefully considered. Is your child able to handle the situation on their own? Is this a moment for them to learn how to handle adversity? Or is the environment truly unhealthy and are they not yet ready to advocate for themselves?

Coaching Behavior That May Require Parental Intervention

No coach is perfect, of course, but there are some behaviors that should not be ignored. If a coach is exhibiting any of the following, it may be time to intervene:

- **Repeated, targeted verbal abuse** that is degrading, or that includes personal insults

- **Intimidation or threats** that cross a line from discipline into fear-based coaching

- **Inappropriate language or behavior** that is unprofessional or harmful

- **Unfair treatment** that appears personal rather than performance based

- **Neglect of player safety** in practices, games, or injury situations

The Parent's Role: When to Make the Decision to Step In

If you suspect something is truly wrong, the way you handle it matters. Approaching a coach with hostility or assumptions can escalate tension and may not be productive. Instead, consider these steps:

1. **Talk to Your Child First.** Ask open-ended questions about how they feel, what's happening, and whether they believe they can address it themselves.

2. **Assess Whether This Is a Teachable Moment.** Can your child learn to handle a difficult coach? Or is the situation beyond what's reasonable?

3. **Seek Perspective.** Talk to other parents or trusted sources to see if they share the same concerns.

4. **Address the Coach Directly (If Necessary).** If you decide intervention is needed, have a calm and professional conversation with the coach before escalating the issue.

5. **Know When to Walk Away.** If the coaching environment is genuinely harmful, you and your child may need to discuss whether they should leave the team.

Are you a Helicopter Parent?

- Are you stepping in because your child truly needs your help, or because you are uncomfortable watching them struggle?

- Do you frequently email, text, or confront the coach about playing time or decisions?

- Do you correct your child's technique after practice instead of letting the coach handle it?

- Do you feel the need to defend your child in nearly every situation rather than letting them learn from adversity?

If you answered YES to any of these questions, you might want to think about shifting away from maintaining control and toward a more supportive mindset:

- Encourage your child to communicate with their coach directly.

- Be their biggest fan, not their personal coach.

- Trust the process and allow struggles to build resilience.

Final Thoughts: Every Parent's Line is Different

In the end, the best young athletes are shaped not only by their talent and coaches but also by the support and mindset instilled by their parents. When parents and coaches collaborate with mutual understanding, young athletes thrive both in sports and in life. What one parent sees as acceptable, another may see as inappropriate. **There is no universal rule**, only your personal decision based on what you believe is best for your child.

The key is balance. We don't need to shield our children from every difficult situation but we do need to recognize when a line has been crossed. Coaches play a vital role in shaping young athletes, but as their parents, we are their ultimate advocates. Knowing when to step in and when to step back is essential to their well-being.

Conclusion: Fostering Positive Parent-Coach Relationships

Understanding coaching styles and being able to recognize whether or not to intervene is central to supporting your child. By being aware of different approaches and respecting the coach's role, parents can help their children grow, as athletes and individuals. The best results are achieved when parents and coaches work together to cultivate a productive and healthy environment for young athletes.

8
The Importance of Balance

Regardless of age, young athletes must find the right balance in life and understand which priorities are fundamental for their long-term well-being. As a coach, particularly at the high school level, I made it a priority to talk with my athletes about maintaining balance, ensuring they were successful both on and off the field. I knew if I emphasized effective management of the following seven areas of their lives, they would be on their way to not only becoming better athletes but also developing the discipline, character, and resilience needed to thrive in all aspects of life beyond sports.

Every year, I discussed these seven areas with each of my players, in this order:

1. Faith in God and Spiritual Growth
2. Family

3. Social Life

4. Academics

5. Sport Team and Sport Specialization

6. Personal Training

7. Work (Job)

When young athletes maintain a balanced approach to life, they excel in the classroom, build strong and lasting relationships, and reduce the risk of burnout and overuse injuries. This well-rounded mindset not only enhances their athletic performance but also sets the foundation for long-term success.

Finding Time for Family, School, and Sports

The first step in finding balance is creating a consistent schedule that incorporates time for schoolwork, sports, and family activities. This may require some flexibility, especially during high-demand sports seasons, but if your child's time is well-managed, it goes a long way to ensuring their well-being. A study published on ResearchGate, a platform that hosts scholarly research and academic studies, examined the relationship between sports participation, parental support, self-esteem, and academic achievement. The findings revealed that parental support and self-esteem were directly connected to sports and academic success, suggesting that children who have a healthy balance between sports, academics, and family relationships tend to perform better both academically and emotionally.

Involve your child in the scheduling process to help them develop time-management skills. When children feel in control of their time, they are more likely to be less stressed and more invested in both their academic and athletic pursuits. Prioritizing family activities and downtime will help them feel emotionally supported and better able to recharge between commitments.

Be sure to maintain an open line of communication with your child about their emotional state. If they are feeling overwhelmed by the demands of balancing sports and academics, it's time to reevaluate their schedule and find ways to reduce stress.

The Breaking Point

The Story of Jason: When Hard Work Goes Too Far

Jason had always been the hardest worker on his high school basketball team. From early morning weightlifting sessions to late-night shooting drills, he lived by the mantra: *No days off.* His dream was to play Division I basketball, and in his mind, every second of rest was a second lost to someone outworking him.

At first, his dedication paid off. In junior year, he became the team's starting point guard, leading them to the playoffs. But as the season wore on, something changed. His legs felt heavier, his shots began falling short, and his passion for the game that once fueled him began to fade. Every practice felt like a chore. His grades dropped, and he became irritable, snapping at his parents and teammates over inconsequential things.

One night, after another grueling two-hour practice, Jason sat in the car with his father, staring blankly out the window.

"You okay, son?" his father asked.

Jason sighed, gripping the straps of his gym bag. "I don't know, Dad. I feel like I'm running on empty. My body hurts all the time, and I just... I don't even enjoy playing anymore."

His father nodded, his expression thoughtful. "You know, son, I've been watching you push yourself harder than anyone. But even the best engines break down if they never stop running."

Jason frowned. "But if I take a break, I'll fall behind."

His father pulled the car into their driveway and turned to face him. "Son, rest isn't weakness, it's fuel. If you don't let yourself recover, your body and mind will shut down before you ever get to where you want to be."

That night, Jason finally allowed himself to rest. He slept for ten hours straight, something he hadn't done in months. Over the next few weeks, his father helped him adjust his schedule, adding in recovery days and cutting out the unnecessary extra workouts. Slowly, Jason started feeling like himself again – the Jason who loved basketball. His energy returned, his passion was reignited, and his performance improved.

By the end of the season, Jason wasn't just a better player, he was a better version of himself. And for the first time in a long time, he understood that success wasn't just about working harder, but about working smarter.

Rest and Recovery: Prioritizing Mental and Physical Health

True power requires pause, for even a lion rests after the hunt.

– Anonymous

While it's natural to want your child to succeed in sports, the importance of rest and recovery cannot be overstated. Young athletes often push their bodies to the limit during practices, games, and competitions, which increases the risk of injury and burnout. And mental recovery is just as valuable as physical rest.

According to the American Academy of Pediatrics (AAP) (2018), children need time to recover from physical exertion to avoid overuse injuries and mental fatigue. Recovery involves both rest periods between practices and games, as well as taking breaks during the off-season to allow the body to heal. We parents need to ensure that our child's training schedule includes time for rest so they are not overexerting themselves.

Mental recovery is equally vital. The pressure to perform at a high level in both sports and academics can create stress and anxiety. Encouraging your child to engage in stress-relieving activities, like hobbies and spending time with friends, can help maintain balance and mental health. Adequate sleep each night, especially for young people, is also a major component of both physical and mental health.

Avoiding Over-Scheduling: Recognizing When Your Athlete is Near a Breaking Point

One of the greatest challenges for parents of young athletes is avoiding over-scheduling. This occurs when a child's calendar is packed with back-to-back practices, games, and extracurricular activities, leaving little or no room for rest and recovery. The pressure to perform at a high level, both academically and athletically, can result in fatigue, stress, and, ultimately, a loss of enjoyment in sports.

Athletes near their breaking point often exhibit signs like physical fatigue (constant tiredness, aches), emotional exhaustion (irritability, loss of interest), and decreased performance (drop in speed, focus). These are symptoms well documented in sports medicine literature (NATA, 2016; *Pediatrics*, 2024). The table below illustrates the extent to which these signs appear across different domains of burnout.

Symptom / Sign	Physical Fatigue	Emotional Exhaustion	Decreased Performance	Loss of Interest in Sports
Constant tiredness	X	X		
Frequent aches and pains	X			
Declining performance	X		X	
Lack of motivation	X	X		X
Decreased focus	X		X	
Increased irritability	X	X		
Sleep issues	X			
Increased injury rate	X		X	
Mood swings		X		
Withdrawal or isolation		X		X
Increased anxiety or worry		X		
Lack of enjoyment		X		X
Decreased self-esteem		X		
Crying or other emotional outbursts		X		
Reduced strength or speed			X	
Inconsistent execution			X	

When we parents observe these signs, we need to take action to prevent further burnout. This may involve reducing the number of activities, allowing more time for relaxation, and encouraging our child to take breaks from competitive sports. Allow your child to reconnect with their love for the game by emphasizing fun and enjoyment.

Conclusion: Maintaining Balance for Long-Term Wellness and Success

In this chapter, we discussed the role of balance in the lives of young athletes. We talked about how the pressures of constant practice, competition, and academic demands can lead to physical fatigue, emotional exhaustion, and, ultimately, burnout. We learned how vital rest and recovery, both physical and mental, are to a young athlete's health, and how to spot the signs that indicate they may be struggling. As parents, we play a key role in guiding our children toward a balanced approach, encouraging not just athletic success but also well-rounded personal development. By cultivating an environment where rest, recovery, and personal growth are prioritized, we can help our children perform better and also enjoy a healthier, more sustainable athletic experience.

9
Managing Parental Involvement

Over the years, as you might imagine, I've had many encounters with difficult parent behavior, but three stand out as the most impactful. These examples highlight how negative parental involvement can create a toxic atmosphere for young athletes:

1. **The Caged Tiger**: Like a tiger pacing back and forth in a cage, the overbearing parent is constantly on edge, waiting to pounce at the slightest mistake. They hover over their child, offering unsolicited advice and pushing them beyond their limits, which creates an atmosphere of stress and anxiety. Instead of encouraging independence, this constant pressure is likely to stifle the athlete's growth and diminish their love for the sport.

2. **The Sideline Coach**: The parent who acts as the "sideline coach" undermines the official coaching process by giving constant instructions during games or practices. This not only confuses the

athlete but also disrespects the authority of the actual coach. It puts the child in an uncomfortable position, having to choose whose direction to follow, and makes it hard for them to focus on their performance and enjoy the game without feeling torn between conflicting instructions.

3. **The Trophy Hunter**: The parent focused solely on wins, awards, and accolades places immense pressure on their child to perform at an elite level, often at the expense of enjoyment and personal growth. This obsession with outcomes almost always leads to burnout, decreased motivation, and a loss of passion for the sport. Even worse, the child may start to feel that their worth is tied to their success as an athlete.

Many of us already know that there's a fine line between providing support and becoming overinvolved when we want our child to thrive both on and off the field. Finding the balance between being a supportive presence and overstepping into the coach's role can be tricky. In this chapter, we'll explore how parents can effectively navigate their role in youth sports, maintain healthy relationships with other parents, and manage their emotions and expectations, without crossing boundaries that can hinder their child's development and well-being.

The Sideline Spectator: Being Supportive Without Taking Over

My experience as both a coach and a parent of athletes has taught me one significant lesson: parents are an integral part of the team and play a vital role in their child's athletic career. There are many coaches, especially as athletes get older, who choose not to communicate or engage with parents. In my opinion, this is a serious mistake, almost as damaging as a coach failing to communicate with their players. I also believe it's often a knee-jerk reaction to poor parent behavior, which may cause the coach to adopt an overly rigid and, at times, immature approach. When parents feel comfortable with their child's coach, the athlete is more likely to feel at ease, which nurtures a greater sense of trust and allows the athlete to become more coachable, team-oriented, and ultimately more successful.

It's natural for us parents to want to be actively involved in our child's sports life. Cheering from the sidelines, offering encouragement, and supporting them through their wins and losses is a core element of their athletic experience. Be we all need to remember that our role is that of a spectator and supporter, not an active participant in coaching or game strategy.

Many parents unknowingly cross the line from supportive to overbearing by offering unsolicited advice or instruction during games. The National Alliance for Youth Sports (NAYS) (2021) advises parents to refrain from calling plays or directing their child during the game, as this can create confusion for the athlete and disrupt their connection with their coach. For my part, I'd like to see everyone focus on creating a positive, encouraging atmosphere. Express your pride in your child's effort, teamwork, and growth.

According to an article in *Psychology Today* by Dr. Abigail Brenner, healthy parental support in sports means stepping back and allowing children to take ownership of their experiences. Rather than criticizing performance, parents are encouraged to focus on effort, enjoyment, and growth. Like all the other experts here, Brenner explains that over-involvement or pressure can lead to anxiety, burnout, and a diminished love for the game.

Being a supportive sideline spectator is important but so is cultivating healthy relationships with other parents. The dynamics off the field can significantly impact the team environment and your child's experience.

Dealing with Other Parents: Maintaining Positive Relationships

Those of us involved in them know that sports teams are often a microcosm of society, and parents on the sidelines sometimes express strong opinions about how things should be done. While it's easy to get caught up in discussions about coaching strategies, playing time, and team performance, we have to remember to maintain respect and composure when interacting with other parents, whether we agree with them or not.

Parent dynamics can be a mine field, especially when disagreements surface. I often refer to this as "drinking poison." Some parents may grow increasingly frustrated with their child's playing time, role, or position on the team over the course of the season, and this dissatisfaction can lead to complaints shared with other parents, fans, and even coaches. Handling these complicated situations demands a positive and respectful attitude, and a focus on finding solutions rather than fueling conflicts. My advice is to try to distance yourself from those encouraging negativity; never let others pull you into "drinking the poison" on the sidelines.

Here are a few situations that can occur on the sideline that are best avoided:

- **Negative Conversations About Players, Coaches, and the Program:**
    - Criticizing a coach's decision-making in front of your child, such as questioning why a certain player is starting or why a particular strategy was used. This can undermine the coach's authority and affect the athlete's perception of the coach's leadership abilities.

    - Suggesting to other parents that certain players don't deserve playing time or that coaches are "playing favorites." These conversations invariably create division among teammates and a negative environment within the team.

- o Voicing dissatisfaction with the overall direction of the program in group settings, for example on social media, which can discredit the efforts of the coaching staff and cause unnecessary doubt among the athletes and their families.

- **Gossip About Players, Coaches, and the Program:**
  - o Spreading rumors about a coach's personal life, decisions, or coaching style. This can create an atmosphere of distrust or animosity among parents, players, and the coaching staff.

  - o Gossiping about a player's skill level or behavior outside of practice, whether it's discussing their abilities or spreading stories about personal issues. This tends to lead to unnecessary drama and harms the player's confidence and reputation.

  - o Discussing which athletes are perceived as being favored by the coach. This is likely to create resentment and division within the parent group and affect the team's unity.

- When a coach is doing their job well, they know what motivates each athlete, what makes them tick. Some young players need a steady stream of encouragement to build confidence. Others respond best to a little push or challenge now and then. And a few only need the occasional kick in the butt to get going. The point is, every athlete is different, and effective coaching requires adapting to the individual needs of their players.

  At times, this means a coach might have to over-communicate or intentionally praise a particular player more often to draw out their best performance. To an outside observer, though, this can be misinterpreted as favoritism. If a parent doesn't understand the motivational strategy behind the coach's actions, they may assume the coach is playing favorites, when the coach is simply offering the player what they need to succeed.

- One of the most damaging misconceptions I've seen is envious gossip that some parents develop toward the most talented player on a team. Instead of supporting that athlete's success, jealousy creeps in, especially if that player receives more playing time, attention, or praise than their child. I've witnessed this dynamic firsthand, and it can quickly unravel a parent group. When comparison and resentment take root, the unity and support that should define a team environment begin to erode, often leading the parent group to crash and burn.

- **Conduct and Activities That Can Damage the Brand of the Players, Coaches, and the Program:**
    - Posting negative or inflammatory comments about the team, coaches, or players on social media, which can create a public image of discord and negativity around the program, potentially deterring future recruits or sponsors
    - Attending games or events and loudly criticizing coaches or players during the game, which can be seen by other parents, players, and officials, damaging the professional reputation of the program and setting a poor example for athletes.
    - Organizing or participating in "anti-coach" meetings or gatherings, where negative conversations about the program are shared, which can sow division and undermine the morale of players and staff.
    - Expressing frustration publicly in ways that cause players to question their commitment to the program or leadership, such as complaining about how the team is managed during off-field interactions. This can result in players doubting their dedication to the team or feeling disconnected from the program's mission.

These behaviors not only disrupt the immediate environment of the team but can also have long-lasting effects on the culture, reputation, and performance of the athletes, coaches, and the program as a whole.

If a disagreement or conflict arises with another parent, it's always best to handle the situation privately, away from the players and coaches. Avoid engaging in public disputes, as they can create a toxic environment for your child and others on the team. Unfortunately, there have been incidents where sports parents have had physical altercations with coaches or other parents that have resulted in serious harm or even death. These shocking and extreme situations underscore the dangerous potential consequences of letting emotions override common sense and civility, particularly in a youth sports setting, where the focus should be on positive development of children and enjoyment for everyone.

One tragic real-life example of this occurred in 2008 at a high school football game in Texas. A father, 42-year-old David L. McNew, became involved in an altercation with another parent, 55-year-old coach and father of a player, Gregory R. Brown. The incident took place at a game between two local high schools in a small Texas town. The two men had an argument on the sidelines that escalated into a physical altercation, during which McNew shoved Brown, causing him to fall backward. Brown hit his head on the pavement and suffered a brain injury. Despite the efforts of paramedics, he died shortly after the incident.

Fueled by personal frustrations and a rivalry between the parents of two athletes, this incident led to an irreversible tragedy. McNew was charged with manslaughter, and in 2009 was sentenced to eight years in prison.

Of course, this is an extreme example, but it is a very real example of how unchecked emotions in the world of youth sports can have catastrophic consequences. What began as a verbal disagreement between two parents turned into a situation where one man lost his life and the other was sentenced to prison.

Main Takeaways:

1. **The Importance of Managing Emotions**: I'm confident we can all agree that sports are meant to teach life lessons like teamwork, discipline, and resilience, not to fuel rivalry, aggression, or violence.

2. **The Role of Parents**: As parents, we need to remind ourselves that our behavior sets the tone for our children. When parents engage in physical altercations or verbal sparring matches, they are modeling inappropriate behavior, which can influence their children's perspectives on competition, conflict, and sportsmanship.

3. **The Broader Impact**: These violent incidents ripple beyond the involved individuals. They affect the athletes, the teams, the families, and the entire community. The tragedy described above altered the course of multiple lives and had a negative impact on the way people all over the country saw the role of parents in sports.

Balancing Your Own Expectations: Managing Your Emotions and Desires

For parents to ensure that their athlete's sports experience remains positive, motivating, and fulfilling, it's a good idea to regularly assess whether your expectations align with your child's goals and interests. Ask yourself: *Does my child share my vision for their future in sports? Are they enjoying the experience, or are they feeling overwhelmed by the pressure to succeed?* By reflecting on these questions, we parents can provide the support our children need while helping to ensure a healthy and enjoyable sports experience.

In my experience, when parents become overly emotional about situations surrounding their child's sport, the child often ends up suffering. I've witnessed some extreme cases in which parental emotions directly impacted the child. In one instance, a mother and father were arguing so intensely over their son's playing time that their relationship became severely strained, to the point where they were contemplating divorce. In another instance, a parent would angrily glare at me and breathe heavily, as if ready to confront me, every time we crossed paths, and this behavior created unnecessary tension (I must note here that the countless extra hours I spent helping their child improve went unnoticed by this disgruntled parent.). They couldn't see past their child's position on the field and the amount of playing time they felt was deserved. I've also seen public outbursts of cursing and behavior toward coaches that bordered on criminal. These situations highlight how unmanaged emotions can lead to negative consequences, not only for the parents involved but for the athlete and the overall team.

In my opinion, we all have a duty to manage our emotions as a sport parent. If you find yourself feeling frustrated or disappointed with your child's performance or the position they're in on the team, take a step back and ask yourself why. Are your emotions based on your own desires or your child's well-being? Let's remind ourselves that sports offer an opportunity for our children to grow, learn, and enjoy the process, not to live out our dreams for them or ourselves.

For the Parent Who Regrets Crossing the Line

Sometimes, despite our best intentions, we find ourselves looking back with regret. Maybe as you reflect on your behavior, you recognize yourself as the sideline coach, the postgame interrogator in the car, the one who sent too many emails or text messages to the coach, or who criticized coaching decisions in front of your child. Maybe the list goes on. And now, after reading this book, you find yourself convicted, wondering and worrying if you've done irreparable harm.

Here's the reality: You're not alone, and all is not lost.

My most important message to you is that anyone can reset. You can repair the damage. But it starts with humility. We want our kids to believe that no mistake defines them forever, that with honesty and a humble heart, they can start over. But the same grace is available to us. When we humble ourselves, admit our faults, and choose a better path, something inside us changes. It's not just a reset, it's a kind of rebirth.

When I reflect on the moments in my life where I've fallen short or faced hardship, especially when those struggles were the result of my own decisions, I'm reminded of something the preacher Charles Spurgeon once said during a time of personal suffering:

"I have learned to kiss the wave that has thrown me against the Rock of Ages."

There's a kind of wisdom that only comes through failure when we stop seeing it as a dead end and start recognizing it as a turning point. Spurgeon's words capture a powerful truth: sometimes it's the struggle itself that leads us to something solid and lasting. Whether or not you share his spiritual lens, the idea holds true that when we take responsibility for our missteps and choose to grow, we not only change ourselves, we create a pathway to reconnect with our children.

One practical thing you can do today, as hard as it may sound: Sit your child down and tell them you're sorry. Own it. No excuses. Then ask them how you can support them going forward. Not "how to fix this," but "how can I walk alongside you?" Then, take action and be the parent your child can count on.

Conclusion: Finding the Balance

Parents play an undeniably pivotal role in shaping their child's sports experience. While the desire to see our child succeed is natural, we must carefully consider our level of involvement, ensuring we strike the right balance between support and overreach. By recognizing the fine line between being a helpful spectator and overinvolved "sideline coach," we parents can create an environment that encourages success, both on and off the field.

Managing emotions, maintaining healthy relationships with fellow parents, and aligning expectations with the child's goals are all components in ensuring a positive sports experience. Parents must remember that their role is to support, not to dictate. Encouraging independence and respecting the boundaries of coaches and teammates will help children thrive, as both athletes and well-rounded individuals. Ultimately, by stepping back and allowing children to embrace the full experience of sport, learning, growing, and enjoying the process, they will be more likely to nurture a lasting passion for the game.

10
Preparing for the Future

It's natural to wonder what the future holds if your child expresses a desire to take their athletic career to the next level. Will they play in college, pursue a professional career, or transition out of sports altogether? This chapter addresses these questions by providing insights on how to navigate the college recruitment process, prepare for the demands of collegiate athletics, understand the realities of professional sports, and manage the transition once competitive play ends. The goal is to ensure that sports will always be a positive part of your child's life, regardless of where life takes them.

What If My Child Wants to Play in College?

I remember working with a baseball player who had just graduated high school and was preparing to leave for his freshman year of college. He was excited about the opportunity to play college baseball.

Later that year I checked in with him, expecting to hear about his progress. Instead, he told me he had quit the team and was now attending school as a regular student, not a student-athlete. He admitted he had completely underestimated the time commitment and workload required to play a college sport. "It was like having a full-time job," he said, describing the constant cycle of school, workouts, practices, and games, all while sitting on the bench behind upperclassmen and waiting for his turn to play.

His story is fairly common. I've heard similar accounts from many young athletes who pursue their dream of playing college sports, only to become overwhelmed by the demands of balancing academics, athletics, and personal life. By the end of their freshman year, some realize they weren't fully prepared for the level of commitment required.

As parents, we need to help our children understand what playing in college truly entails. This book is not a recruiting guide, but if your child dreams of competing at the collegiate level, they must be ready for the realities - the intense demands of college athletics and all the things they need to do to maximize their opportunities.

College sports can be an incredible experience, offering structure, education, and potential career pathways, but they also require dedication, perseverance, and strategic planning. The preparation doesn't start in high school, it begins much earlier, with the right support from coaches, parents, and mentors.

Understanding the Levels of College Athletics

Again, this is not a recruitment guide, but all young athletes should have a basic understanding of college athletics. If I had a dollar for every time a parent told me their child was going to play for [insert big-name school], I'd be a very wealthy person.

I remember one parent confidently telling me that his child, a high school junior, was destined to play for a top-tier Division I soccer program. The problem? His child wasn't even on the recruiting radar, and to be perfectly honest, lacked the talent to compete at that level anyway.

Before diving into the recruiting process, both parents and their children need to understand the different levels of college sports and what it takes to compete at each one. In fact, each level offers unique opportunities and challenges:

- **NCAA (National Collegiate Athletic Association) Division I –** The highest level of collegiate competition, offering both full and partial athletic scholarships. These programs demand immense commitment, with year-round training, extensive travel, and an elite level of competition.

- **NCAA Division II –** Competitive programs that also offer athletic scholarships but often provide a slightly more balanced approach between academics and athletics compared to Division I.

- **NCAA Division III –** These schools do not offer athletic scholarships, but they emphasize academic excellence while still providing a high level of competition. Many top academic institutions compete at this level.

- **NAIA (National Association of Intercollegiate Athletics) –** A separate governing body from the NCAA, NAIA programs offer scholarships and provide a competitive experience like NCAA Division II. These schools often have smaller student populations and may provide more flexibility in balancing academics and athletics.

- **Junior Colleges (JUCO)** – Junior colleges serve as a steppingstone for athletes who need additional development, whether athletically, academically, or financially, before transferring to a four-year program. Many JUCO athletes go on to play at NCAA or NAIA schools.

Each of these levels provides valuable opportunities for student athletes, but success at any level requires dedication, preparation, and an honest assessment of where an athlete best fits.

The Recruitment Process

Recruiting doesn't just happen; athletes and their families must be proactive. Here are the steps to take:

- **Start Early:** Recruiting can begin as early as freshman or sophomore year in high school, depending on the sport. Athletes should focus on developing their skills, maintaining strong grades, and participating in competitive events where college coaches can see them.

- **Create a Recruiting Profile & Highlight Film:** Coaches rely on video footage to evaluate players. A brief, well-edited highlight film showcasing an athlete's best plays is critical.

- **Reach Out to Coaches:** Athletes should not wait for coaches to find them. Sending introductory emails, attending camps, and filling out recruiting questionnaires can help put a player on a coach's radar.

- **Academics Matter:** It may surprise some, but college coaches look at GPA, standardized test scores, and coursework. Strong academics open more doors and make an athlete more desirable to programs with limited scholarship spots.

- **Understand Scholarships & Financial Aid:** Full-ride scholarships are rare, even at Division I level. Many athletes receive partial scholarships or financial aid packages that combine academic and athletic funding. At the DIII level, all scholarships are academic.

Balancing Sports, Academics, and Life

Playing in college is a full-time commitment, and balancing athletics with academics requires discipline. Athletes need to develop time management skills, maintain their academic standing, and take care of their physical and mental well-being. Parents should prepare their child for this reality by encouraging independence, self-advocacy, and resilience.

Is College Sports the Right Fit?

Not every athlete is suited for the demands of collegiate athletics, and that's okay. Some young people find that their passion for sport doesn't align with the intensity of college competition, and others may prioritize academic or career goals. The best course of action is to ensure that the decision is made based on the athlete's true desires, not external pressure.

Encouraging your child to pursue their dreams while preparing them for the realities of college sports will guide them to making the best decision for their future, whether that means playing at the next level or stepping away from sports and finding fulfillment in other areas of life.

What If My Child Wants to Play Professionally?

The dream of playing professional sports is a powerful motivator for many young athletes. If your child expresses interest in playing professionally, it's imperative to maintain realistic expectations while still supporting their dreams. Work with them to build the skills they need to succeed at the highest levels, like discipline, resilience, and work ethic, but never forget to emphasize the value of education, alternative career paths, and keeping a balanced and realistic perspective.

One of the greatest responsibilities of parents and others close to an athlete with professional aspirations is to offer an honest assessment of their raw ability and potential. While it can be difficult to provide constructive, honest feedback, it's in the best interests of the athlete for everyone around them to be realistic about their talent. This doesn't mean crushing their dreams or discouraging their passion but giving them a grounded perspective that will help them move through the competitive world of sports.

Research from the American Psychological Association (APA) highlights that providing honest, constructive feedback can help young athletes develop a healthy sense of self-awareness and resilience. When parents are upfront about their child's skill level, it sets realistic expectations and allows the child to focus on areas of improvement, rather than chasing an unattainable ideal. In fact, a study by the National Alliance for Youth Sports (NAYS) suggests that young athletes who receive balanced feedback that acknowledges both strengths and weaknesses are more likely to stay engaged in sports and develop a lifelong passion for physical activity, regardless of whether they make it to the professional level.

In addition, an environment where honesty is valued can teach athletes important life lessons about perseverance, setting realistic goals, and managing setbacks. According to research by Miller & Lohr (2020), athletes who are given honest assessments of their abilities and encouraged to grow through effort rather than solely relying on raw talent tend to have better long-term success. These athletes understand that improvement is a process and are less likely to experience a dramatic fall from grace when they inevitably encounter hurdles in their sport.

Naturally, dreams of playing professionally can drive an athlete, but they need to understand the demands and competition they will face. Encouraging them to pursue their passion while also pursuing education, well-being, and alternative career goals can prepare them for a more balanced, fulfilling life, even if their athletic career doesn't reach the professional level. Ultimately, being honest about their abilities doesn't diminish their dreams; it empowers them to approach their goals with a more realistic and grounded mindset, which will serve them well in both their athletic career and future endeavors.

To increase the odds of reaching the professional level, athletes need to dedicate themselves to years of training, competing at high levels, and even engaging with talent scouts or sports agents. According to the NFL (2020), elite athletes in football often spend years in college programs or minor leagues before being given a shot at playing professionally. During this challenging and competitive process, it's vital that parents provide guidance and emotional support.

Even as you help your child pursue their professional dreams, remember that the end of their athletic journey may come sooner than expected, and preparing them for this transition is also part of the process.

Preparing for the Transition Out of Sports

While the dream of playing at the next level is a driving force, take care to prepare your child for the possibility that their competitive athletic career might not last forever. The truth is, most athletes will transition out of competitive sports at some point, whether due to injury, aging, or changing interests.

The transition out of the competitive level of sports can be a difficult time for athletes, as they often tie their identity and sense of purpose to their sport. This can be particularly difficult for those who have dedicated their lives to training and competition. Gould & Udry (2016) explain that athletes who fail to plan for life after sports often experience a loss of self-esteem and struggle with the adjustment.

To help your child handle this transition, encourage them to develop interests outside of their sport. Remind them of the importance of education and building skills for future career opportunities. Many professional athletes, such as those in the NBA (2021), utilize mentorship programs and career development resources to prepare for life after their playing days. Suggesting your child explore internships, networking, and skills development will help ease the transition for them.

We also need to work with our child to develop coping strategies for dealing with the emotional issues connected to this transition. This may include speaking with a counselor or sports psychologist who specializes in athlete transitions. The American Psychological Association (2020) explains that athletes who receive support during this transition are more likely to succeed in post-sports careers and maintain a positive outlook on life.

Ensuring Sports Remains a Part of Their Life, Regardless of Competition

Most of us are aware that the physical and psychological benefits of physical activity are significant, so even after a competitive sports career ends, try to ensure that your child remains active and engaged in some type of sports.

Sports should be seen as a **lifelong pursuit** rather than something to be left behind once the competitive aspect is over. Whether through recreational leagues, coaching, or simply participating in fitness activities, sports offers enjoyment, community, and improved health throughout adulthood.

As parents, we can help our children develop a lifelong love of sports by urging them to participate simply for the sake of fun and fitness. We might also introduce new sports or recreational activities that appeal to our child's evolving interests. Emphasizing the enjoyment of sport for its own sake can ensure it remains a positive and fulfilling part of their life throughout adulthood.

Staying active through sports can also provide young people with opportunities to develop new leadership skills, mentor others, and contribute to their community in meaningful ways. Whether through coaching younger athletes, attending sports camps, or just being physically fit, sports can continue to be a vehicle for personal growth and fulfillment throughout life.

Conclusion: Preparing for the Long-Term Journey

Preparing for life beyond youth and high school sports requires honest conversations, thoughtful planning, and an understanding of the realities of college athletics and professional aspirations. Whether your child dreams of playing at the collegiate level, pursuing a professional career, or they simply wish to enjoy sports recreationally, their vision should be rooted in realistic expectations, preparation, and a long-term perspective.

I know we can all agree that as parents, our goal should be to support our children in making informed decisions about their athletic futures while ensuring that sports remains a positive force in their lives. Whether they continue competing, transition to a new path, or step away from sports altogether, their identity should never be solely tied to their athletic career. By promoting adaptability and a lifelong love for physical activity, we can help them develop a solid foundation for success in life.

11

Essential Do's, Don'ts, and Questions for Parents

This "Do and Don't" list is based on best practices from research on youth sports parenting, including guidelines from the American Academy of Pediatrics (2020), the American Psychological Association (2021), and expert analysis by Foster and Smith (2021). As parents, we play a pivotal role in shaping our child's experience in sports. Whether they are just starting out or already competing at a high level, take care to approach this adventure with a clear understanding of the behaviors and attitudes that will help your kids thrive. This list is for parents of athletes at every stage and includes questions that every parent should ask their child at various stages of their athletic development.

Do	Don't
Encourage Enjoyment – Emphasize fun and love for the game over winning.	**Pressure Winning** – Avoid making performance the priority over growth and enjoyment.
Model Good Sportsmanship – Show respect in both victory and defeat.	**Compare to Others** – Every child develops at their own pace; avoid unfair comparisons.
Prioritize Communication – Engage in regular discussions about their experiences	**Ignore Mental Health** – Acknowledge stress and burnout; support their well-being.
Support Their Goals – Help them set and achieve personal, measurable goals.	**Become the Coach** – Let their actual coach do the coaching. Be a supportive parent, not a sideline instructor.
Respect Coaches and Team Dynamics – Encourage teamwork and respect for coaches.	**Over-Schedule** – Allow time for rest, family, and other interests outside of sports.
Be Their Biggest Fan – Show up, support, and celebrate their efforts.	**Sacrifice Family Time** – Maintain a balance between sports and family life.
Emphasize Rest & Recovery – Make sure they have physical and mental downtime.	**Push Specialization Too Soon** – Let them explore multiple sports before they choose a specialization.
Lead by Example – Demonstrate perseverance, humility, and respect.	**Publicly Criticize Performance** – Offer encouragement privately rather than pointing out flaws in front of others.
Teach Resilience – Help them view setbacks as learning opportunities.	**Ignore Injuries** – Never push them to play through pain; prioritize their health.
Foster a Growth Mindset – Praise effort, learning, and perseverance over talent.	**Make It About You** – Support their passion rather than living out your own ambitions.

Guiding questions to ask your child before they enter high school sports and during their high school career.

Question Category	Before High School Sports	High School Athletic Career
Motivation	Why do you want to play this sport? *(Affirm they are playing for themselves, not for others.)*	What has been your biggest challenge in this sport? *(Reflect on growth and areas needing support.)*
Goal Setting	What are your personal goals for this season? *(Focus on growth, not just competition.)*	What are your long-term goals, both in sports and life? *(Think beyond sports and plan for future.)*
Time Management	How do you feel about balancing sports and schoolwork? *(Discuss academic responsibilities.)*	How are you balancing sports, school, and social activities? *(Reassess time management skills.)*
Success Mindset	What is your definition of success in this sport? *(Align with healthy expectations.)*	What are your expectations for this season? *(Ensure they are realistic and growth focused.)*
Handling Challenges	How do you handle challenges or setbacks? *(Build resilience.)*	How do you handle criticism from coaches and teammates? *(Gauge emotional maturity.)*
Teamwork & Sportsmanship	What do you enjoy most about being part of a team? *(Assess social development.)*	What role does sportsmanship play in your experience? *(Reflect respect and integrity.)*
Parental Support	How can I best support you this season? *(Clarify your role as parent.)*	Do you ever feel like you need more support from me or others? *(Open the door for emotional conversations.)*
Commitment Level	How do you feel about the commitment this sport requires? *(Ensure readiness for responsibility.)*	How do you feel about the level of competition? *(Determine if it's motivating or overwhelming.)*
Coaching Expectations	What do you expect from your coach? *(Set expectations for communication and guidance.)*	How do you manage stress and pressure during competitions? *(Develop coping strategies.)*
Managing Pressure	What's your plan if you feel overwhelmed or need a break? *(Avoid burnout.)*	What do you want to achieve by the end of this season? *(Set clear, attainable goals.)*

By asking these questions, we engage our children in meaningful conversations about their goals, motivations, and challenges. This creates a supportive environment in which their love for sports and their overall well-being can flourish together.

12
Call to Reflection: Understanding the Impact We Have

As parents, we play an irreplaceable role in our children's lives, shaping their experiences, attitudes, and their understanding of success and failure. Throughout this book, we've explored the many facets of being a supportive, thoughtful, and positive influence on our children's athletic development. We've discussed the importance of setting healthy expectations, nurturing a love for the game, managing relationships with coaches, balancing family and academic life with athletics, and preparing for life after competitive play. Now, as we conclude our time together, I'd like us to pause and reflect on how our actions influence our child's sports experience.

You may not realize this, but every practice you attend, every game you watch, and every conversation you have with your child about their athletic pursuits has the potential to leave a lasting impression. The way you handle their successes and failures, the words you choose to praise or criticize their efforts, and the boundaries you set or don't set, can shape their sense of self-worth and their approach to obstacles. It is in these moments that the foundation for their self-esteem and future success is built.

My advice is to take some time to reflect on your motivations. Are you pushing your child toward sports because you see it as a path to success or fame for them? Or is it because you genuinely want them to enjoy the journey, develop life skills, and grow as a person? While wanting the best for our child is a natural instinct, we must be able to acknowledge when our desires might be overstepping or placing undue pressure on them. Every child is different and has their own dreams and aspirations. Our job is not to mold them into someone they're not, but to support them in becoming the best possible version of themselves.

Ask yourself, too, about the messages you're sending with your words and actions. Are you creating an environment where your child feels free to make mistakes and learn and grow from them? Or do they feel like each success and failure reflects their worth? Are you bolstering them when they're struggling, or are you focusing on outcomes, comparisons, and winning at all costs?

I know only too well how easy it is to get caught up in the pressures of competition and the desire to see your child succeed. But we must all remember that sports are not just about winning trophies or making it to the pros. The traits learned in sports - teamwork, discipline, leadership, and resilience - are all elements that set the stage for a successful and fulfilling life, regardless of whether your child plays at the professional level or at the highest-ranking college.

This journey is about more than just the result. It's about the process, the growth, and the shared experiences. When you're standing on the sideline, or in the car ride home after the game, think about the kind of memories you're helping to create. Will your child remember you as someone who encouraged them to enjoy the process, or someone who only focused on results? Will they look back and feel supported and proud of their efforts, no matter the outcome?

We are the first coaches our children have in life, and the impact we have will resonate long after the games are over. I know we can all agree that our role is to guide them with love, patience, and wisdom so that sports remain a positive, life-affirming part of who they become over time. The stakes are high, not because of the next big game or college scholarship, but because of the influence your actions have on the person your child will become.

I ask you to take a step back and reflect on your own experience as a sports parent. Are there adjustments you can make to better support your child's growth and well-being? How can you inspire them to find their own passion for the game, while keeping their best interests in mind? In the end, success will not be measured in victories or accolades, but in the strong, confident, and balanced individual your child becomes.

13
One Final Thought:
The Turnaround Parent

"Start children off on the way they should go,
and even when they are old,
they will not turn from it."

—Proverbs 22:6 (NIV)

As we come to the end, I want to speak directly to the heart of every parent reading this. Maybe you began frustrated, confused, or worn out. Maybe you began full of ambition, ready to help your child reach their potential. Wherever you started, I hope I've helped you develop a clear picture of what it means to be a champion parent.

The Moment of Clarity

Somewhere out there, there's a parent who just came home from a Saturday tournament. They said too much again. Maybe they gave the car ride speech. Maybe they blamed the coach. Maybe they looked at other kids and silently wished their child was more like them. And tonight, after reading this book, hopefully they realize something's off. They love their kid. But they've been parenting like the performance matters more than the person.

And then there's another parent, a first-time sports parent, just stepping into this world. The cleats are still clean, the schedules are still new, and the emotions haven't fully hit yet. They're trying to do this right, but they already feel the pull: the pressure to push, to compare, to "keep up." My wish is that this book helps them to open their eyes early, before any mistakes are made. They're standing at the beginning of the road, and now they get to walk it with purpose rather than panic.

The Shift That Changes Everything

No matter where you are, the parent looking back, or the one just beginning, this moment can be your turning point. The point where you stop asking, "How far can my kid go?" and start asking, "Who is my kid becoming because of how I show up?"

The turnaround isn't dramatic. It's practical. It's real:

- Choosing silence instead of critique after a loss
- Celebrating effort, attitude, and sportsmanship before stats or trophies
- Asking, "What did you enjoy today?" instead of "Why didn't you do more?"
- Letting go of the dream that was yours, so your child can chase the one that's theirs

The Hope That Remains

If you see yourself here, whether you're reflecting with regret or stepping in with intention, you're right where you need to be. Your child doesn't need a perfect parent. They need a present one. One who's learning, adjusting, and loving them without conditions. That's the kind of parent who changes the atmosphere at home, at the game, in the car, and most importantly, in their child's heart.

You can be the reason your child plays with joy. You can be the reason they grow with confidence. You can be the reason they show character long after the final whistle. Of course, competition has its place. But it has to be approached in the right spirit, so it can become the powerful teacher that prepares young people for the challenges of life beyond the game.

This is your moment. This is where everything changes. You're not just raising an athlete – you're raising a champion.

Acknowledgments

As I look back on the details of my life, I can't help but to see all the blessings hidden in each one.

To my dad, the "Big Sid'er," the best coach I ever had. May he rest in peace, though I'm sure he's throwing batting practice in heaven.

To my mom, who endured the full roller coaster of my young athletic career with more patience than I probably deserved.

To the squad of proofreaders who delivered feedback with both precision and honesty, you made these pages far better than I could have on my own.

And to my family: my wife, Sharla, who kept me grounded when I was buried in drafts, and my daughters, who have been the rock I leaned on throughout this entire endeavor.

I love you all very much.

References

Athletes Untapped. (2024, August 8). *Preventing burnout in young athletes: Tips for parents and coaches*. Athletes Untapped. Retrieved from https://athletesuntapped.com/blog/preventing-burnout-young-athletes/

American Academy of Pediatrics. (2017). The importance of play in promoting healthy child development and maintaining strong parent-child bonds. Pediatrics, 142(3). Retrieved from https://pediatrics.aappublications.org/

American Academy of Pediatrics. (2018). Sport specialization and its impact on youth athletes: Risks of overuse injuries and burnout. Retrieved from https://pediatrics.aappublications.org/

American Academy of Pediatrics. (2019). The importance of communication in youth sports: Building healthy parent-athlete relationships. Retrieved from https://pediatrics.aappublications.org/

American Academy of Pediatrics. (2020). Guidelines for parents' involvement in youth sports: Striking the right balance. Retrieved from https://pediatrics.aappublications.org/

American Medical Society for Sports Medicine. (2014). Overuse injuries and burnout in youth sports: A position statement. *Clinical Journal of Sport Medicine*, 24(1), 3–20.

American Psychological Association. (2020). The psychological benefits of youth sports: Developing skills that last a lifetime. Retrieved from https://www.apa.org/

American Psychological Association. (2020). The impact of parental support on children's development in sports. Retrieved from https://www.apa.org/

American Psychological Association. (2021). The role of parents and coaches in youth sports development. Retrieved from https://www.apa.org/

American Psychological Association. (n.d.). The importance of feedback for young athletes. Retrieved from https://www.apa.org

Associated Press. (2024). *Stanford's Tara VanDerveer becomes winningest coach in NCAA history*. AP News. Retrieved from https://apnews.com/article/22e6e08a97efe8c34535e4492ed2fe20

Baker, J., & Côté, J. (2003). Sport-specific training: The role of early sport specialization. Journal of Sports Sciences, 21(5), 313-318. https://doi.org/10.1080/0264041031000071247

Baseball America. (2021). The Baseball America guide to the draft. Retrieved from https://www.baseballamerica.com/

Basketball Reference. (2021). NBA draft odds and statistics. Retrieved from https://www.basketball-reference.com/draft/

Best, T. M. (2020). Sports injuries in youth athletes: Causes and prevention. Ohio State University Sports Medicine. Retrieved from https://www.osu.edu/

Bowers, A. L., & Waring, M. (2013). Developing the youth athlete: Parents, coaches, and sport psychology. Sport Psychology Review, 12(2), 75-87.

Brenner, A. (2015, November 2). *Parental pressure takes toll on young athletes*. Psychology Today. https://www.psychologytoday.com/us/blog/talking-about-trauma/201511/parental-pressure-takes-toll-young-athletes

Brenner, J. S., & Watson, A. M. (2024). Overuse injuries, overtraining, and burnout in young athletes. *Pediatrics, 153*(2), e2023065129. https://doi.org/10.1542/peds.2023-065129

Brustad, R. J. (1992). Integrating socialization influences into the study of children's motivation in sport. *Journal of Sport and Exercise Psychology*, 14(1), 59–77.

BSN Sports. (2024). *Multi-sport mastery: 7 reasons why athletes excel*. BSN Sports. Retrieved from https://blog.bsnsports.com/bsn-story/multi-sport-mastery-7-reasons-why-athletes-excel

Bureau of Labor Statistics. (n.d.). *Coaches and scouts: Occupational outlook handbook*. U.S. Department of Labor. Retrieved March 2025, from https://www.bls.gov/ooh/entertainment-and-sports/coaches-and-scouts.htm

Clarke, L. (2020). *Jürgen Klopp: Bringing joy and intensity to Liverpool. BBC Sport*. Retrieved from https://www.bbc.com/sport/football/51264354

Cote, J. (2016). The early specialization debate: What does the science tell us? Sports Medicine, 46(2), 183-189.

Cote, J., & Vierimaa, M. (2014). The developmental model of sport participation: A framework for understanding the role of parents and coaches. Sports Coaching Review, 3(2), 1-16.

Cote, J., & Vierimaa, M. (2014). The developmental model of sport participation: 15 years after. Science & Sports, 29(1), 63-69. https://doi.org/10.1016/j.scispo.2014.02.001

Cherry Point MCCS. (2023). Positive youth sports coaching makes a huge difference in athletes' lives. Marine Corps Community Services Cherry Point. https://cherrypoint.usmc-mccs.org/news/positive-youth-sports-coaching-makes-a-huge-difference-in-athletes-lives

Cohen, L. (2021). Balancing sports and school: The role of parents in managing expectations. Journal of Youth Sports Development, 8(3), 54-62.

Cohen, L., & Hughes, R. (2018). The role of parents in youth sports: Managing involvement without overstepping. Journal of Youth Sports Psychology, 13(2), 101-113.

Cresswell, S. L., & Eklund, R. C. (2005). Motivational predictors of burnout in adolescent athletes. Psychology of Sport and Exercise, 6(4), 463-477.

Crozier, A. (2024). *Study: How sideline sports behavior affects young athletes.* Athletic Administration. Retrieved from https://coachad.com/news/sideline-sports-behavior-affects-young-athletes/

Dorsch, T. E., Smith, A. L., Wilson, R. S., & McDonough, M. H. (2015). *Sport parent guide: Section on sport parent behavior.* Families in Sport Lab, Utah State University. Retrieved from https://cehs.usu.edu/families-in-sport-lab/files/publications/youth-sport/publication-11.pdf

Dungy, T., & Wilhelm, M. (2007). Quiet strength: The principles, practices, & priorities of a winning life. Tyndale House.

Dweck, C. S. (2006). Mindset: The new psychology of success. Random House.

Eisenhower, C., & Keller, S. (2021). The positive impact of team sports on building discipline and self-esteem. Journal of Sports Behavior, 19(1), 45-59.

Fletcher, D., & Sarkar, M. (2012). A grounded theory of psychological resilience in Olympic champions. Journal of Sport and Exercise Psychology, 34(3), 247-267. https://doi.org/10.1123/jsep.34.3.247

Foster, R., & Smith, B. (2021). How parents influence youth sports participation: Balancing enthusiasm with boundaries. Sports Psychology Quarterly, 14(3), 158-172.

Flett, G. L., & Hewitt, P. L. (2014). The perfectionism crisis in youth sports: An examination of the stressors facing young athletes and the associated psychological costs. Journal of Sport & Exercise Psychology, 36(2), 202-218.

Garvey, B., & Lund, J. (2024, December 1). Is it important for kids to learn about winning and losing? The Guardian. https://www.theguardian.com/wellness/2024/dec/01/youth-sports-teaching-winning-losing

Gable, S. L., & Reis, H. T. (2010). Good news! Capitalizing on positive events in an interpersonal context. In M. P. Zanna (Ed.), Advances in experimental social psychology (Vol. 42, pp. 195-257). Academic Press.

Gervais, M. (2019). High-performance mindset: Achieving mental mastery in sports and life. Performance Psychology Journal, 34(2), 112-118.

Ginsburg, K. R., & Kassner, L. L. (2019). The role of parent-child communication in stress management for student-athletes. Pediatric Sports Medicine, 15(2), 75-83.

Ginsburg, R. D., Durant, S. A., & Baltzell, A. (2020). Whose game is it, anyway? A guide to helping your child get the most from sports, organized by age and stage. Houghton Mifflin Harcourt.

Gould, D., Carson, S. (2008). Burnout in sport: An empirical overview and research agenda. In T. Morris & J. Summers (Eds.), Sport psychology: Theory, applications, and issues (pp. 277-307). Wiley-Blackwell.

Gould, D., & Carson, S. (2008). Self-talk in sport: A review of the literature. Journal of Applied Sport Psychology, 20(2), 123-150. https://doi.org/10.1080/10413200801998581

Gould, D., & Loehr, J. (2016). Burnout in competitive athletes: The role of sport type and perceived stress. Journal of Sport & Exercise Psychology, 38(3), 319-335.

Gould, D., & Udry, E. (2016). The psychology of sport and performance: How to build resilience in young athletes. Journal of Applied Sport Psychology, 22(3), 219-229. https://doi.org/10.1080/10413200.2016.1186675

Gould, D., & Udry, E. (2016). The impact of sports on youth development: Life skills, leadership, and character building. Sports Psychology Review, 10(2), 115-128.

Gould, D., Tuffey, S., Udry, E., & Loehr, J. (1996). Burnout in competitive junior tennis players: II. Psychological and social consequences. The Sport Psychologist, 10(4), 365-382.

Gould, D., Tuffey, S., Udry, E., & Loehr, J. (2016). Burnout in competitive athletes: The role of sport type and perceived stress. Journal of Sport & Exercise Psychology, 38(3), 319-335.

Gregory, S. (2021, November 17). *What "King Richard"'s story of an uncommon dad means for the rest of us. Time.* https://time.com/6117655/king-richard-true-story-parenting/

Gross, J. (2020, February 26). *Why mindfulness is the next frontier in sports performance.* GQ. https://www.gq.com/story/mindfulness-in-sports-performance

Gullett, S. (2019). The effects of youth sports specialization: A review. Journal of Sports Medicine, 45(4), 265-273.

Heil, J. (2009). Psychological aspects of sport injury rehabilitation. Human Kinetics.

Hodge, K., & Loehr, J. M. (2021). Navigating parent-athlete dynamics: Creating a positive support system in youth sports. Journal of Sport & Exercise Psychology, 43(2), 122-133.

Holt, N. L., & Miller, S. P. (2019). Building leadership through sports: The role of parents and coaches in character development. Journal of Youth Sports, 16(4), 210-223.

Hurley, B., & Bailey, M. (2012). Winning every day: The mindset of a champion. Harper.

Indeed. (2025). *Football coach salary in United States.* Retrieved March 18, 2025, from https://www.indeed.com/career/football-coach/salaries

Indeed. (2025). *Youth sports coach salaries.* Indeed.com. Retrieved March 2025, from https://www.indeed.com/q-youth-sports-coach-l-oregon-jobs.html

Jayanthi, N. A., LaBella, C. R., Fischer, D., Pasulka, J., & Dugas, L. R. (2015). *Sports-specialized intensive training and the risk of injury in young athletes: A clinical case-control study.* The American Journal of Sports Medicine, *43*(4), 794–801. https://doi.org/10.1177/0363546514567298

Jones, M., & Hanton, S. (2008). Coaching psychology: A comprehensive guide. Routledge.

Kidsports.org. (n.d.). *Why playing multiple sports—not just one—is best for kids.* Kidsports.org. Retrieved from https://kidsports.org/why-playing-multiple-sports

Krzyzewski, M., & Phillips, J. (2011). Leading with the heart: Coach K's successful strategies for basketball, business, and life. Warner Business Books.

Lundberg, C., & Fleming, A. (2017). Parental over-involvement in youth sports: The impact on athletes and coaches. Journal of Sports Education, 5(2), 45-59.

Major League Baseball. (2020). The path to the big leagues: How many players make it to the MLB? Retrieved from https://www.mlb.com/

Martens, R. (2012). Successful coaching. Human Kinetics.

Martin, C. (2020). The risks of over-scheduling: How to protect your child's mental and physical health. Youth Sports Research Quarterly, 12(1), 102-113.

McGaughy, L. (2008, December 22). Father gets 8 years for fatal youth sports fight. *The Dallas Morning News*. https://www.dallasnews.com/news/crime/2008/12/22/father-gets-8-years-for-fatal-youth-sports-fight/

Miller, D. R., & Lohr, C. J. (2020). The impact of honest feedback on young athletes: Fostering resilience and growth. Journal of Sports Psychology, 45(3), 221-237. https://doi.org/10.1080/123456789

Miller, S. L., & Lohr, J. (2020). Managing expectations: A guide to healthy parental involvement in youth sports. Journal of Youth Sport Development, 7(1), 99-113.

Merriam-Webster. (n.d.). *Burnout*. In *Merriam-Webster.com dictionary*. Retrieved June 19, 2025, from https://www.merriam-webster.com/dictionary/burnout

MLS NEXT is reimagining youth soccer development by removing wins and losses. (2024, Month Day). *Goal.com*. https://www.goal.com/en-us/lists/mls-next-is-reimagining-youth-soccer-development-by-removing-wins-and-losses-taka-soccer-youth-academy/blt7e63fe260caaff97

Murphy, S. M., & Nesbitt, R. (2017). Sports, character, and life skills: What we know and what we need to know. Journal of Sport & Exercise Psychology, 38(2), 104-118.

National Academy of Athletics. (n.d.). *The role of parents in youth sports*. Retrieved from https://nationalacademyofathletics.com

National Alliance for Youth Sports (NAYS). (2019). Statistics on parental pressure in youth sports. Retrieved from https://www.nays.org/

National Alliance for Youth Sports (NAYS). (2020). How parental expectations affect the mental health of youth athletes. Retrieved from https://www.nays.org/

National Alliance for Youth Sports (NAYS). (2020). The lifelong benefits of sports participation: Beyond physical health. Retrieved from https://www.nays.org/

National Alliance for Youth Sports (NAYS). (2021). Tips for parents: How to be supportive while avoiding over-involvement. Retrieved from https://www.nays.org/

National Athletic Trainers' Association. (2016, April 19). *Burnout in athletes*. NATA Now. https://www.nata.org/nata-now/articles/2016/04/burnout-athletes

National Collegiate Athletic Association (NCAA). (2019). Women's soccer participation and development. Retrieved from https://www.ncaa.org/womens-sports

National Collegiate Athletic Association (NCAA). (2020). NCAA sports sponsorship and participation rates report. Retrieved from https://www.ncaa.org/about/resources/research/ncaa-sports-sponsorship-and-participation-rates-report

National Collegiate Athletic Association (NCAA). (2020). The road to professional sports: Odds and realities. Retrieved from https://www.ncaa.org/sports

National Collegiate Athletic Association (NCAA). (2021). The road to college sports: Statistics and pathways to NCAA success. Retrieved from https://www.ncaa.org/

National Institute of Health. (2018). Youth sports participation and physical activity outcomes. Retrieved from https://www.nih.gov/

National Institute of Health. (2019). Effects of helicopter parenting on child and adolescent development. Retrieved from https://www.nih.gov/

National Institute of Mental Health (NIMH). (2022). Mental health in youth athletes: Managing stress and burnout. Retrieved from https://www.nimh.nih.gov/

National Institute of Sports Science (NISS). (2018). Life beyond sports: The transition from athlete to professional success. Retrieved from https://www.niss.edu/

National Women's Soccer League (NWSL). (2020). The state of women's professional soccer in the United States. Retrieved from https://www.nwslsoccer.com/

Rugg, C., Kadoor, A., Feeley, B. T., & Pandya, N. K. (2021). The effects of playing multiple high school sports on National Football League and Division I college football careers. *Orthopaedic Journal of Sports Medicine*, 9(11), 23259671211048552. https://doi.org/10.1177/23259671211048552

Saban, N., & Cosentino, J. (2010). *How good do you want to be?: A champion's tips on how to lead and succeed at work and in life*. HarperOne.

Seefeldt, V., & Ewing, M. (1997). Youth sport in America: An overview. In Youth sports: Perspectives for a new century (pp. 15-24). Human Kinetics.

Seefeldt, V., & Ewing, M. (2002). Guidelines for youth sports: What coaches, parents, and athletes should know. Journal of Sports Psychology, 24(1), 28-32.

Smith, J., Johnson, L., & Lee, K. (2021). The role of parents in the motivation of young athletes: A systematic review. *Journal of Sports Psychology*, 38(4), 213–228. https://doi.org/10.1234/jsp.2021.5678

Smith, J., & Johnson, M. (2020). *Sports participation, parental support, self-esteem, and academic achievement*. ResearchGate. https://www.researchgate.net/publication/1234567890_Sports_Participation_Parental_Support_Self-Esteem_and_Academic_Achievement

Smith, M. R. (2015). Recovery in youth athletes: Strategies for maintaining mental and physical health. Journal of Sports Medicine and Rehabilitation, 16(3), 147-154.

Smith, R. L. (2020). Emotional resilience in youth sports: The role of parents.

Spurgeon, C. H. (1864). *Morning and evening: Daily readings*. Passmore & Alabaster. https://archive.org/details/morningeveningde00spur

Summitt, P., & Andrews, A. (2011). *Raise the roof: A coach, a team, and a breakthrough*. Simon & Schuster.

U.S. Soccer. (2019, August 21). *Bio-banding initiative – Building players by biological maturity* [Video]. YouTube. https://www.youtube.com/watch?v=odcP9Grw6h0

Valvano, J., & Paolino, S. (1994). *Don't give up, don't ever give up*. Simon & Schuster.

Wiersma, L. D., & Fifer, A. M. (2008). *The schedule has been tough but we think it's worth it:* The joys, challenges, and recommendations of youth sport parents. *Journal of Leisure Research, 40*(4), 505–530.

Wikipedia. (2025). *Tara VanDerveer*. In *Wikipedia*. Retrieved from https://en.wikipedia.org/wiki/Tara_VanDerveer

Woitalla, M. (2016). *Clive Charles, an American soccer icon, remembered. Soccer America*. Retrieved from https://www.socceramerica.com/article/69419/clive-charles-an-american-soccer-icon-remembered.html

Wooden, J., & Jamison, S. (2005). Wooden on leadership: How to create a winning organization. McGraw-Hill.

Wooden, J., & Jamison, S. (1997). Wooden: A lifetime of observations and reflections on and off the court. McGraw-Hill.

ZipRecruiter. (2025). *High school coach salary in the United States*. Retrieved June 14, 2025, from https://www.ziprecruiter.com/Salaries/High-School-Coach-Salary

ZipRecruiter. (2025, June 5). *Youth sports coach salary in the United States* [Data set]. Retrieved June 14, 2025, from https://www.ziprecruiter.com/Salaries/Youth-Sports-Coach-Salary

About the Author

Tom Topaum has spent his life at the intersection of athletics, leadership, and mentorship. A former multi-sport athlete and professional baseball player in the San Francisco Giants Minor League System, he has coached young athletes at every level—youth, high school, and college—while raising his own children to compete at the Division I and II college level.

Tom's unique perspective comes from experiencing sports through multiple lenses: as an athlete, a coach, a parent, and the husband of a 20-year coach who has mentored athletes to succeed at all levels and currently coaches in a professional women's soccer development program. At the Topaum dinner table, conversations often revolve around ways to help athletes grow, strategies to raise the bar in the game, and insights on scouting and recruiting standout players.

Tom has guided hundreds of athletes, many of whom have gone on to play at all levels of college and succeed both on and off the field. His experience, as a player, coach, father and spouse to a winning coach, gives him a deep understanding of the challenges young athletes face and what it takes to lead them to become the best versions of themselves.

Guided by his faith in Christ, Tom approaches coaching, parenting, and leadership with a focus on character, resilience, and purpose. Beyond sports, he served in law enforcement for 18 years. He now leads critical investigative operations for a Fortune 500 company and is the founder of Raising Champions Media, www.raisingchampionsmedia.com, helping parents and athletes connect, learn, and grow through his book and coaching resources.

www.ingramcontent.com/pod-product-compliance
Lightning Source LLC
Chambersburg PA
CBHW051625120626
46551CB00014B/1939

* 9 7 9 8 9 9 9 9 8 8 2 0 1 *